ANALYZING THE ISSUES

CRITICAL PERSPECTIVES ON
WHISTLEBLOWERS
AND LEAKERS

Edited by Rita Santos

Enslow Publishing

101 W. 23rd Street
Suite 240
New York, NY 10011
USA

Published in 2019 by Enslow Publishing, LLC
101 W. 23rd Street, Suite 240, New York, NY 10011

Library of Congress Cataloging-in-Publication Data

Names: Santos, Rita, editor.
Title: Critical perspectives on whistleblowers and leakers / edited by Rita Santos.
Description: New York : Enslow Publishing, 2019. | Series: Analyzing the issues | Includes bibliographical references and index. | Audience: Grade 7-12.
Identifiers: LCCN 2018002886| ISBN 9780766098602 (library bound) | ISBN 9780766098619 (pbk.)
Subjects: LCSH: Whistle blowing—United States—Juvenile literature. | Leaks (Disclosure of information)—United States—Juvenile literature.
Classification: LCC JF1525.W45 C75 2019 | DDC 353.4/60973—dc23
LC record available at https://lccn.loc.gov/2018002886

Printed in the United States of America

To Our Readers: We have done our best to make sure all website addresses in this book were active and appropriate when we went to press. However, the author and the publisher have no control over and assume no liability for the material available on those websites or on any websites they may link to. Any comments or suggestions can be sent by email to customerservice@enslow.com.

Excerpts and articles have been reproduced with the permission of the copyright holders.

Photo Credits: Cover, Rena Schild/Shutterstock.com; cover and interior pages graphics Thaiview/Shutterstock.com (cover top, pp. 1, 4-5), gbreezy/Shutterstock.com (magnifying glass), Ghornstern/Shutterstock.com (interior pages).

CONTENTS

INTRODUCTION

W hen employees witness illegal or unethical behavior on behalf of their employer they have two choices: to ignore it or to report it. Those who choose to report are known as whistleblowers or leakers. While most whistleblowers are legally protected from retaliation, not all are. Federal employees are exempt from whistleblower protection laws because of their handling of classified information. Public opinion on whistleblowers changes based on the individual and the type of information they disclosed.

In 2010, Private Chelsea Manning was responsible for leaking American military documents to the website Wikileaks. The documents could have compromised the safety of some soldiers in the field but also revealed the true extent of civilian casualties in the Iraq and Afghanistan wars. The documents also showed evidence of the use of torture on Iraqi civilians. It was one of the largest leaks in the nation's history, with more than 700,000 documents being published online.

To many, Manning was a hero. She alerted the nation to the human rights violations the military was engaging in and the true costs of the war. Others, including the US Justice Department, saw her as a traitor who had threatened national security. Manning was convicted of seventeen of twenty-two charges, including some violations of the Espionage Act. After seven years behind bars, President Obama commuted the remainder of her sentence in 2016.

The case of Chelsea Manning shows the intricacies of whistleblowers. The US military claimed the leak was a threat to national security but also could not name anyone who was hurt as a direct result of the leaked information. Some see her lengthy prison sentence as justice served while others see it as unjust retaliation. Manning paid a high personal price for being a whistleblower. While some of the information she revealed did lead to public outcry and diplomatic embarrassment for the United States, it seemed to have little effect on the war in Iraq.

The act of whistleblowing is surrounded by ethical questions with no easy answers. Is it ethical to leak confidential information that proves proof of wrongdoing, like Manning did, even though it could potentially cause harm to others if released? What kind of information is in the public's best interest to know? Different sectors of society have different responses to these kinds of questions. Academics and social scientists are attempting to answer the ethical questions surrounding whistleblowers through research and study, while the courts and politicians grapple with the questions based on legal precedent or ideology.

It is in a government's best interest for the information it deems "classified" to remain so, however, what's in a government's best interests isn't always what's best for the people. The government must walk a fine line between protecting certain information that keeps the nation safe while still encouraging people to come forward when they see wrongdoing. To this end, the US government tries to make going to the media the last resort for any federal employee who needs to report on something concerning. It has also passed laws that protect most employees from retaliation for whistleblowing.

The media also struggles with the complexity of leaked information. Whistleblowers can make for great headlines, but reporters have an ethical duty to ensure the validity of any claims they print and to protect the safety of their sources and the public. During the 1970s, reporters at the *New York Times* released portions of classified documents known as "The Pentagon Papers," which proved the government had lied about its actions in the Vietnam War. The reporters had to be careful to print what the public needed to know without putting national security at risk. Their source, Daniel Ellsberg, was initially charged with conspiracy, espionage, and theft of government property, but the charges were dropped.

Whether people are blowing the whistle on their employers or a government agency, they need to know their legal rights. Organizations like the National Whistleblower Center and the Sunlight Foundation strive to help people understand the ethics of leaking and protect those who do. They also work to educate the public on the need for whistleblowers.

In this book, you will hear what people from different critical perspectives have to say on the topic of whistleblowers. It is a topic every citizen should put some thought into. As you read, think about what it would take for you to become a whistleblower—and what protections you would like to have in place if ever you needed to become one.

CHAPTER 1

WHAT THE ACADEMICS SAY

Whistleblowing often brings unethical, illegal, and potentially dangerous situations to light. However, there are times when exposing information does more harm than good. It is the work of academics and researchers to explore the ethical issues involved in whistleblowing. Many journalists and researchers are interested in finding ways to encourage whistleblowing that will keep people safe and discourage the leaking of information, like troop locations, which could have deadly consequences in the wrong hands. However, not everyone agrees about when leaks are necessary. One way researchers state that companies can deal with leaks is to offer strong whistleblower protections that allow the company to deal with it internally before being leaked to the press. Without such laws in place, whistleblowers currently face steep consequences for coming forward, even when the majority of people feel their actions were ethically justified.

"TRUTH AND CONSEQUENCES: LESSONS FROM WORLDCOM," BY ALAYNA ALVAREZ, FROM, *THE TEXAS ENTERPRISE*, JUNE 12, 2013

Groupthink. Rationalization. Fear. These are just some of the psychological hurdles faced by would-be whistleblowers when they make the decision to expose corporate wrongdoing.

Cynthia Cooper, the former vice president of the internal audit group at WorldCom, knows a thing or two about being caught up in workplace ethical dilemmas. In 2002 she was the key whistleblower in her company's $3.8 billion accounting fraud case, which at that time was the largest instance of corporate fraud in history.

Cooper — author of "Extraordinary Circumstances: The Journey of a Corporate Whistleblower" and one of Time magazine's three People of the Year in 2002 — now travels the nation to share her tumultuous experiences during the onset and aftermath of the WorldCom crisis.

Speaking at McCombs in April as part of the Ethics and Corporate Social Responsibility Speaker Series, Cooper explained the factors that lead otherwise ethical people to cheat or commit fraud. Corporate conflicts have now become so common, she said, that employees need to strengthen their ethical judgment so they are ready when the time comes to make tough choices.

"It's important to prepare yourselves now for the ethical dilemmas you'll face in the workplace," said Cooper. "Because it's not if — it's when."

CUTTING CORNERS

Cooper's story unfolded in a time when WorldCom's stock value and earnings were on the decline, putting pressure on the firm to deliver better results for investors.

In 2000, two of the company's mid-level managers, Betty Vinson and Troy Normand, encountered a significant ethical dilemma. They were five days away from having to release earnings to the public, and there was an error in the books they couldn't resolve: The line costs expense had jumped up dramatically and was completely out of line with the company's revenues. The expenses had been moved from the income statement to the balance sheet, cutting it as an asset to make the company seem more profitable.

Troubled and feeling the pressure of the approaching deadline, the two managers confronted Former WorldCom CFO Scott D. Sullivan. Instead of providing direct answers, he instructed Vinson and Normand to cover up the mistake by drawing on excess reserves. That way, everything would seemingly be aligned with the expectations of external auditors and Wall Street analysts, and they could be given time for the error to "reveal itself in future quarters."

Sensing their uneasiness and growing guilt, the CFO began praising their work and appealing to their loyalty.

Cooper said Sullivan's pep talk went something like this: "He said, 'Look, guys — I want you to think of this as an aircraft carrier: We've got planes out. Let's get all the planes landed safely. Once all the planes have landed safely, then if you want to leave the company, you can leave. … No one's going to prison. If anyone were going to prison, it would be me. You're just following orders.'"

Fearful of losing their jobs and financial security for their families, Vinson and Normand followed the orders of their superior, changing the numbers on the balance sheet and hiding the truth from the public.

"DIFFICULT TO STOP"

In the months that followed, Sullivan planned to fix the problem through accounting tricks. But to do so, he needed Cooper to delay her internal audit. Growing suspicious of her superior's increasing persistence, Cooper withstood the pressure to play along.

Once Sullivan realized the auditor would not back down, he decided to come clean, justifying his poor decisions by telling her "it was difficult to stop" cooking the books after the first time he manipulated the numbers.

Cooper didn't buy it, and with the help of her internal auditing team, she sniffed out the discrepancies and became one of the world's most famous whistleblowers.

Vinson and Sullivan received prison sentences of six months and five years, respectively, and Normand received three years of probation. WorldCom CEO Bernard Ebbers is still serving a 25-year term for his role in the fraud.

RISKS, REWARDS AND REPERCUSSIONS

The decision to come forward did not come easily to Cooper, as she contemplated the potential repercussions of her actions. Despite some high-profile exceptions — such as the IRS' record $104 million award to UBS whistleblower Bradley Birkenfeld last fall — corporate truth-tellers don't always come out on top.

Most whistleblowers end up leaving their companies (voluntarily or involuntarily) within a year of speaking up, and many others suffer through hardships such as long-term unemployment, financial instability, anxiety, alcoholism, social isolation, and marital problems. Cooper, who experienced depression and major weight loss throughout the ordeal, described the experience as "by far the most difficult thing I've ever been through."

"It was literally all I could do but get out of bed and put one foot in front of another," she said. "I realized I had a choice to make. I could either let this ruin my life or I could try and find a way through it and do something completely new."

Cooper still feels empathy for the managers, board members, auditors, and other employees who were working at WorldCom at the time — even those who were involved in the scandal.

"The people who were complicit with the fraud were not just numbers to us—they were people who we had worked with for many years," Cooper said. "Nobody wakes up and says, 'I want to become a criminal today.' It's a slippery slope, and people go down that slope one step at a time."

"We all have the power of choice," she added. "You can give it away, but you all have the power of choice, so prepare yourselves."

1. Are people morally obligated to become whistleblowers?

2. Why did Cynthia Cooper become a whistleblower?

"KNOWING WHEN TO BLOW THE WHISTLE," BY JEREMY SIMON, FROM *THE TEXAS ENTERPRISE*, JUNE 10, 2013

If your company wants to be alerted to internal wrongdoing, it takes more than offering your employees an anonymous whistleblower hotline, according to experts at the McCombs School of Business.

In the case of National Security Agency whistleblower Edward Snowden, the government certainly did not want the whistle blown publicly on their surveillance programs. But within companies, corporate executives usually want to hear about internal problems, says McCombs Lecturer Grace Renbarger, who spent four years as the chief ethics and compliance officer at Dell.

"They can't stop it if they don't know about it," she says.

Many large companies offer mechanisms such as ethics hotlines that enable workers to anonymously report misconduct. Under the Sarbanes-Oxley Act, which was passed in 2002, all publicly traded companies must have mechanisms for the reporting of accounting or audit fraud.

But those hotlines don't always get used. According to NPR, research from the University of

Michigan shows that as many as one in five workers report observing violations of their companies' code of conduct, even though only half of the employees spoke up about the violations.

Why don't more employees report wrongdoing? One problem could be a corporate culture that discourages it. To get more employees to speak up, "you have to tackle the culture itself," says Associate Professor of Management Ethan Burris.

WHISTLEBLOWING ISN'T EASY

The consequences of becoming a whistleblower are "generally pretty awful," says Robert Prentice, professor and interim chair of the Business, Government, and Society department.

Prentice explains that whistleblowers are often shunned by coworkers, may be fired, and can have difficulty finding work in their industry ever again.

Some companies require whistleblowers to file an internal report before they can go to outside regulators, such as the Securities and Exchange Commission, at the risk of being discredited by their employer. Unemployment, combined with years spent in court battling former employers, can drag whistleblowers into bankruptcy. In the most extreme cases, whistleblowers may be the victims of physical intimidation or even murder. There is speculation, for example, that the 1974 death of nuclear safety activist Karen Silkwood may have been linked to her public opposition to unsafe practices at her company.

"Being a whistleblower is far from rosy," Prentice says.

Things may not turn out so great for the company, either. Employee whistleblowing can potentially mean fines, lawsuits or government investigations of the company, Prentice says. If the whistleblowing case isn't handled well internally or high-level executives are involved, expect the press to pick up on it. "You're going to hear a lot of publicity about the really catastrophic ones," Renbarger says.

Just ask the NSA.

INTERNAL MECHANISMS

For companies, it's important to get workers to speak up before problems get too serious.

Companies should consider how they are soliciting employee input. Renbarger says most large U.S. corporations have toll-free hotlines or Web portals managed by third-party vendors that allow employees to blow the whistle while remaining anonymous.

Some experts say more needs to be done. Anonymous hotlines are important "symbolic actions," but they aren't enough, says Burris, who researches how employees share feedback in the workplace. "To me, that is really just sticking a Band-Aid on the underlying issue," Burris says.

A hotline doesn't change the wider corporate culture that not only allowed wrongdoing to occur, but also made the employee feel the need to seek out an independent third party, either inside or outside the organization, to resolve the issue, Burris says.

CHANGING CORPORATE CULTURE

Instead, Burris says employees should be talking about serious workplace problems with their managers. The company can encourage discussion by letting workers know that it's safe and worthwhile to speak up about sensitive issues, and by letting managers know that it's safe and worthwhile to address problems and make changes, rather than continuing with the status quo.

"Unless you have both pieces involved, you're not really going to change the equation all that dramatically for employees," Burris says.

Renbarger agrees that corporations need to set the proper tone.

"If the culture is one of openness and transparency, that values integrity and encourages people to speak up, then I think there will be more reporting," she says. "On the other hand, if the culture is authoritarian, greed-obsessed, and lacking in values, then there will be a lot less reporting because people are either afraid or don't care — they just want to keep their heads down, get their paycheck, and go home."

Burris' research has shown that to get employees talking, managers should be physically present, open and nice about receiving employee feedback, and willing to take action when appropriate. They also should let employees know how their feedback is being used — or not used — and why. Most importantly, managers need to visit employees on their turf and request input, rather than waiting for employees to come to them.

In other words, touting your open-door policy doesn't mean much on its own, Burris says. "Unless you actually do something with [employee feedback], why would I want to waste my time going out of my way and sticking my neck out to tell you how things really are if nothing is going to change?"

For companies that want their employees to speak up, hiring good management isn't enough, though. Employers need to take a holistic approach to the corporate culture, since the company as a whole has a greater influence than the malleable personalities of individual managers.

"If the culture's terrible, they're going to adapt to that terrible culture," Burris says.

1. Should companies offer strong whistleblower protections?

2. What keeps people from becoming whistleblowers?

"WHEN IS A LEAK ETHICAL?," BY CASSANDRA BURKE ROBERTSON, FROM *THE CONVERSATION*, JUNE 12, 2017

Twenty-five-year-old Reality Leigh Winner remains in jail after a federal judge denied her bail in a case where she is alleged to have sent classified information to the media. Winner faces up to 10 years in prison if convicted.

Winner's prosecution comes at a time when the Trump administration has been faced with numerous leaks of sensitive information. The White House has stepped up efforts to identify leakers. And the Justice Department has also vowed to crack down on them. The Obama administration similarly took a hard line on leakers, prosecuting them more aggressively than any presidential administration in the last 40 years. Winner is the first person to be criminally charged for leaking by the current administration.

Undoubtedly, leaking classified information violates the law. For some individuals, such as lawyers, leaking unclassified but still confidential information may also violate the rules of professional conduct.

But when is it ethical to leak?

PUBLIC INTEREST DISCLOSURES

I am a scholar of legal ethics who has studied ethical decision-making in the political sphere.

Research has found that people are willing to blow the whistle when they believe that their organization has engaged in "corrupt and illegal conduct." They may also speak up to prevent larger threats to cherished values, such as democracy and the rule of law. Law professor Kathleen Clark uses the phrase "public interest disclosures" to refer to such leaks.

Scholars who study leaking suggest that it can indeed be ethical to leak when the public benefit of the information is strong enough to outweigh the obligation to keep it secret.

A LANDMARK CASE

The case of Jesselyn Radack illustrates the ethical concerns that go into the decision to leak publicly. Radack served as an ethics advisor in the Justice Department under President George W. Bush. When American John Walker Lindh was captured in Afghanistan in December 2001, allegedly fighting on behalf of the Taliban, Radack advised the department that interrogating Lindh without allowing him to have a counsel present would violate attorney ethics rules and could jeopardize his prosecution. Her advice was ignored.

When Lindh was criminally charged, prosecutors were supposed to turn over any internal communications about the case. But Radack found that her earlier emails concluding that Lindh's interrogation was unlawful had "disappeared from the office file while the Justice Department was under a court order to produce it." This led Radack to believe that the department had failed to turn over the information.

As a result, Radack leaked the relevant emails to *Newsweek*. After Radack's legal advice became public, the government agreed to a plea bargain with Lindh. Lindh would serve 20 years in prison instead of the "three life sentences plus another 90 years" that he could have gotten if he lost at trial.

Radack faced significant personal challenges as a result of leaking. She was the subject of a criminal investigation (though never formally charged), underwent a 10-year-long professional disciplinary investigation by the bar and was even placed on a security watchlist that "triggered secondary searches at every airport."

Radack went on to have a career specializing in providing legal representation to others charged with making unauthorized leaks. Ultimately, Radack's work in whistleblowing earned her a major award for protecting the First Amendment.

LEAKING A LARGE AMOUNT OF DATA

Radack's disclosure was limited to a single case. But some of the most controversial leaking cases in recent years have involved what law professor Margaret Kwoka has termed "deluge leaks" that disclose huge amounts of data at once.

Edward Snowden, for example, leaked "hundreds of thousands of top-secret documents" relating to government surveillance programs. Chelsea Manning, a U.S. army soldier, also leaked hundreds of thousands of documents, including classified diplomatic cables, "to reveal what she believed were atrocities on the part of the U.S. government." Manning spent more than seven years in prison, while Snowden sought refuge in Russia to avoid prosecution.

Both Snowden and Manning expressed a commitment to ethical ideals. However, I would argue that because of the broad scope of their leaks, the disclosures had the potential to cause greater harm than more limited leaks – an important factor that scholars weigh in when measuring the ethics of leaking. According to political science professor Jason Ross Arnold, for example, Manning's disclosures may have helped enemies "plan targets and develop strategies" to harm Americans. The U.S. government also spent millions of dollars trying to rebuild intelligence assets in the wake of Snowden's revelations.

FIGHTING LEAKS

Attorney General Jeff Sessions has said that "it will probably take some convictions to put an end" to leaks from the Trump administration. But a look at the motivation of leakers suggests that criminal prosecution alone will not plug the flow of leaks.

Radack, Snowden and Manning have all said they were aware they could face serious consequences for leaking. But they were willing to take that chance because they thought it was more important to expose what they saw as serious wrongdoing. The threat of criminal or professional sanctions did not deter them.

Encouraging internal whistleblowing may be a more effective way to prevent leaks.

Researchers have found that a robust internal process may be a key factor in preventing leaks. It is common for people to try to work within the system before leaking to the public. It is when higher-ups acknowledge illegal conduct but refuse to do anything about it, or when individuals suffer retaliation for bringing concerns up the internal chain of command, that leakers may believe that the only ethical choice is to go public.

We don't know Reality Winner's motivation for leaking or whether she will face criminal consequences for her alleged leaks. But when the decision to pass on information stems from a sense of ethical obligation, leakers will often accept serious personal risks to bring that information to the public.

1. When do you consider it ethical to become a whistleblower?

2. When do you consider it unethical to become a whistleblower?

"WHAT IS CLASSIFIED INFORMATION, AND WHO GETS TO DECIDE?," BY JEFFREY FIELDS, FROM *THE CONVERSATION*, MAY 16, 2017

Before coming to academia, I worked for many years as an analyst at both the State Department and the Department of Defense.

I held a top secret clearance, frequently worked with classified information and participated in classified meetings. Classified information is that which a government or agency deems sensitive enough to national security that access to it must be controlled and restricted. For example, I dealt with information related to weapons of mass destruction and their proliferation.

Handling written classified information is generally straightforward. Documents are marked indicating classification levels. It is sometimes more difficult to remember, however, whether specific things heard or learned about in meetings or oral briefings are classified. Government employees sometimes reveal classified details accidentally in casual conversations and media interviews. We may not hear about it because it's not in the interviewee's or employee's interest to point it out after the fact, or he or she may not even realize it at the time.

In 1991, Sen. David Boren accidentally revealed the name of a clandestine CIA agent during a news conference. At the time, Boren was no less than chairman of the Senate Select Committee on Intelligence.

Not all revelations of classified details are earth-shattering, like nuclear launch codes. Many are rather mundane. A former colleague of mine who was a retired CIA analyst used to tell his students he would never knowingly, but almost certainly would inadvertently, share a tidbit of classified information in the classroom. It is very difficult to remember many "smaller" details that are sensitive.

Dealing with large amounts of classified information over a career increases the possibility of accidentally sharing a small nugget. Sharing classified information knowingly, or revealing information one should know is sensitive, is a different matter.

Here's how the system of classification works.

CLASSIFICATION LEVELS AND CONTENT

The U.S. government uses three levels of classification to designate how sensitive certain information is: confidential, secret and top secret.

The lowest level, confidential, designates information that if released could damage U.S. national security. The other designations refer to information the disclosure of which could cause "serious" (secret) or "exceptionally grave" (top secret) damage to national security.

At the top secret level, some information is "compartmented." That means only certain people who have a top secret security clearance may view it. Sometimes this information is given a "code word" so that only those cleared for that particular code word can access the information. This is often used for the most highly sensitive information.

There are several other designators that also indicate restricted access. For example, only those holding a secret or top secret clearance, and the critical nuclear weapon design information designation, are allowed to access information related to many aspects of the operation and design of nuclear weapons.

It is common for written documents to contain information that is classified at different levels, including unclassified information. Individual paragraphs are marked to indicate the level of classification. For example, a document's title might be preceded with the marker (U) indicating the title and existence of the document is unclassified.

Within a document, paragraphs might carry the markers "S" for secret, "C" for confidential or "TS" for top secret. The highest classification of any portion of the document determines its overall classification. This approach allows for the easy identification and removal of classified portions of a document so that less sensitive sections can be shared in unclassified settings.

NOT QUITE CONFIDENTIAL

Below the confidential level, there are varying terms for information that is not classified but still sensitive.

Government agencies use different terms for this category of information. The State Department uses the phrase "sensitive but unclassified," while the Department of Defense and the Department of Homeland Security use "for official use only." These markers are often seen in the headers and footers of documents just like classified designations.

WHO DECIDES?

Executive Order 13256 spells out who specifically may classify information.

Authority to take certain pieces of information, say the existence of a weapons program, and classify it top secret is given only to specific individuals. They include the president and vice president, agency heads and those specifically designated by authorities outlined in the executive order.

Procedures for declassification of materials are complicated. They are delineated in Executive Order 12356. However, the president has ultimate declassification authority and may declassify anything at any time.

Deciding what information is classified is subjective. Some things clearly need to be kept secret, like the identity of covert operatives or battle plans. Other issues are not as obvious. Should the mere fact that the secretary of state had a conversation with a counterpart be classified? Different agencies disagree about issues like this all the time.

In practice, when people leave the government they often engage in media interviews, write books and have casual conversations. There are bound to be complications and revelations – accidental or otherwise.

1. What are the differences between the three levels of classification?

2. Who decides what is classified? What are the challenges of deciding how information is classified?

"THE WIKILEAKS CIA RELEASE: WHEN WILL WE LEARN?," BY RICHARD FORNO AND ANUPAM JOSHI, FROM *THE CONVERSATION*, MARCH 8, 2017

This week's WikiLeaks release of what is apparently a trove of Central Intelligence Agency information related to its computer hacking should surprise no one: Despite its complaints of being targeted by cyberattackers from other countries, the U.S. does a fair amount of its own hacking. Multiple federal agencies are involved, including the CIA and the National Security Agency, and even friendly nations. These latest disclosures also remind us of the cybersecurity truism that any electronic device connected to a network can be hacked.

As cybersecurity researchers conducting a preliminary review of the data released in what WikiLeaks calls "Vault 7," we find the documents mostly confirm existing knowledge about how common hacking is and how many potential targets there are in the world.

This round of leaks, of documents dating from 2013 to 2016, also reinforces perhaps the most troubling piece of information we already knew: Individuals and the government itself must step up cyberdefense efforts to protect sensitive information.

ALMOST EVERYTHING IS HACKABLE

For years, security experts and researchers have warned that if something is connected to the internet it is vulnerable to attack. And spies around the world routinely gather intelligence electronically for diplomatic, economic and national security purposes.

As a result, we and others in the cybersecurity community were not surprised by the 2013 revelations from former NSA contractor Edward Snowden. We knew that the spying programs he disclosed were possible if not likely. By contrast, the general public and many politicians were astounded and worried by the Snowden documents, just as many citizens are surprised by this week's WikiLeaks disclosure.

One element of the new WikiLeaks "Vault 7" release provides more insight into the scope of government spying. In a project called "Weeping Angel," CIA hackers and their U.K. counterparts worked to turn Samsung F8000 smart television sets into remote surveillance tools. Hacked TV's could record what their owners said nearby, even when they appeared to be turned off.

The fact that the CIA specifically targeted smart televisions should serve as yet another a wake-up call to the general public and technology manufacturers about cybersecurity issues inherent in modern devices. Specifically, "smart home" and Internet of Things devices represent a massive vulnerability. They are open to attack not only by government organizations seeking intelligence on national security information, but terrorists, criminals or other adversaries.

It's not necessarily a good idea to have always-on and network-enabled microphones or cameras in every room of the house. Despite many of these devices being sold with insecure default settings, the market is growing very rapidly. More and more people are buying Google Home or Amazon Echo devices, Wi-Fi enabled baby monitors and even internet-connected home-security equipment.

These have already caused problems for families whose devices overheard a TV newscaster and ordered dollhouses or whose kids were tracked by a teddy bear. And large parts of the internet were disrupted when many "smart" devices were hijacked and used to attack other networked systems.

PHONES WERE A KEY TARGET

The CIA also explored ways to take control of smartphone operating systems, allowing the agency to monitor everything a phone's user did, said or typed on the device. Doing so would provide a way around post-Snowden encrypted communications apps like WhatsApp and Signal. However, some of the CIA's methods of attack have already been blocked by technology vendors' security updates.

The CIA's apparent ability to hack smartphones casts doubt on the need for officials' repeated calls to weaken mobile phone encryption features. It also weakens the government's claim that it must strengthen surveillance by not telling tech companies when it learns of security weaknesses in everyday products. Just like the door to your house, technological vulnerabilities work equally well in providing access to both "good guys" and "bad guys."

Ultimately, as a society, we must continue to debate the trade-offs between the conveniences of modern technologies and security/privacy. There are definite benefits and conveniences from pervasive and wearable computing, smart cars and televisions, internet-enabled refrigerators and thermostats, and the like. But there are very real security and privacy concerns associated with installing and using them in our personal environments and private spaces. Additional problems can come from how our governments address these issues while respecting popular opinion and acknowledging the capabilities of modern technology.

As citizens, we must decide what level of risk we – as a nation, a society and as individuals – are willing to face when using internet-connected products.

WE'RE FREQUENT ATTACKERS – BUT BAD DEFENDERS

The WikiLeaks release also reconfirms a reality the U.S. might prefer to keep quiet: While the government objects to others' offensive cyberattacks against the United States, we launch them too. This isn't news, but it hurts America's reputation as a fair and aboveboard player on the international stage. It also reduces American officials' credibility when they object to other countries' electronic activities.

Leaks like this reveal America's methods to the world, providing plenty of direction for adversaries who want to replicate what government agents do – or even potentially launch attacks that appear to come from American agencies to conceal their own involvement or deflect attribution.

But perhaps the most disturbing message the WikiLeaks disclosure represents is in the leak itself: It's another high-profile, high-volume breach of information from a major U.S. government agency – and at least the third significant one from the secretive intelligence community.

Perhaps the largest U.S. government data loss incident was the 2014 Office of Personnel Management breach that affected more than 20 million current and former federal workers and their families (including this article's authors). But the U.S. has never truly secured its digital data against cyberattackers. In the 1990s there was Moonlight Maze; in the 2000s there was Titan Rain. And that's just for starters.

Our government needs to focus more on the mundane tasks of cyberdefense. Keeping others out of key systems is crucial to American national security, and to the proper function of our government, military and civilian systems.

Achieving this is no easy task. In the wake of this latest WikiLeaks release, it's certain that the CIA and other agencies will further step up their insider-threat protections and other defenses. But part of the problem is the amount of data the country is trying to keep secret in the first place.

We recommend the federal government review its classification policies to determine, frankly, if too much information is needlessly declared secret. Reportedly, as many as 4.2 million people – federal employees and contractors – have security clearances. If so many people need or are given access to handle classified material, is there just too much of it to begin with? In any case, the information our government declares secret is available to a very large group of people.

If the U.S. is going to be successful at securing its crucial government information, it must do a better job managing the volume of information generated and controlling access to it, both authorized and otherwise. Granted, neither is an easy task. However, absent fundamental changes that fix the proverbial cult of classification, there likely will be many more WikiLeaks-type disclosures in the future.

1. What privacy concerns surround smart devices?

2. How did Snowden's information about the NSA change how people view technology?

"ETHICAL JOURNALISM: WHAT TO DO - AND NOT TO DO - WITH LEAKED EMAILS," BY FRANZ KRÜGER, FROM *THE CONVERSATION*, JUNE 11, 2017

South Africans have been gripped by stories gleaned from the biggest data dump in the country — between 100,000 and 200,000 emails leaked by an anonymous source to journalists. The emails, locally referred to as the "Gupta leaks", reveal how the Gupta family has done business in the country, as well as their engagements with the government and politicians. The family, and its associates, are accused of buying favor, as well as state tenders and deals, through their close association with President Jacob Zuma, members of his family and politicians loyal to him. The Conversation's Ozayr Patel asked Professor Franz Krüger how journalists should respond to leaks of this kind.

WHAT ARE THE ETHICAL QUESTIONS JOURNALISTS SHOULD ASK THEMSELVES WHEN REPORTING ON LEAKED INFORMATION, PARTICULARLY BULK LEAKS SUCH AS THESE EMAILS?

It is important for journalists to satisfy themselves that the leaked information is real, and to seek as much corroboration as possible.

The second question that needs consideration is whether and how the leak furthers a political or other agenda. We have been very accustomed in South Africa to see political warfare by leak, and journalists should not allow themselves to be misused in factional battles. But this is a secondary question to the one about whether the information is true and in the public interest. If the leaked information stands up as accurate, and if it is important for the general public to know, it would be reasonable to publish even if it furthers somebody's interest.

In a situation of that kind, though, it is important for the political background to the leaks to be contextualized.

Another issue that arises from the sheer volume of material that seems to have been leaked is how to pace the release of the various stories. In this case, the material has generated a lot of different kind of revelations, which have been published over time. Some of these have been stronger than others.

What are the four things every journalist should do when covering leaks of this kind?

Check the information, consider alternative explanations, consider the political and factional context of the leaks taking place, allow the people implicated a full and proper chance to respond.

WHAT ARE THE FOUR THINGS EVERY JOURNALIST SHOULD DO WHEN COVERING LEAKS OF THIS KIND?

Check the information, consider alternative explanations, consider the political and factional context of the leaks taking place, allow the people implicated a full and proper chance to respond.

IS THE REPORTING OF THE LEAKED EMAILS BEING HANDLED IN AN ETHICAL WAY?

In general, I think it has been. I was a bit concerned that in one case, there seems to have been a policy not to ask for a response, and I don't think that is appropriate. The country's press code does allow that in some cases, but they are exceptional, and I don't think in this case the danger of publication being prevented is strong enough.

I also feel that some of the stories published were overplayed – more was made of them than seemed really justified. Also, in some cases too much may have been read into the raw information available. It's sometimes easy to read things into exchanges that may in fact be quite innocent, particularly where they seem to confirm a narrative that is increasingly accepted as common cause.

In general, though, the reports have given the public a sense of the detailed texture of state capture which was not available before.

WHAT ARE THE DANGERS OF "LEAK FATIGUE"?

There is a danger with any particular kind of reporting that audiences will get tired of it, and will switch off. It's well known that there is "confession fatigue" where the public gets tired of stories of suffering.

Journalists need to be alive to that possibility, and avoid getting too taken up by their own interests and passions to notice that ordinary audiences sometimes have different priorities. The risk is simply that audiences will lose interest, particularly if a perception develops that a story is being milked beyond what is relevant or interesting. The stories chosen need to be significant.

WHAT ARE THE DANGERS THAT JOURNALISTS WILL LOSE THEIR CREDIBILITY?

Credibility is very important to journalism. The central reason to worry about ethics in this – and in other cases – is to safeguard credibility. Despite some weaknesses, I have not picked up a sense in the public discussion that, in general, these stories are sensationalized and that therefore journalists involved should worry about their credibility.

1. What questions should journalists ask themselves before deciding to report on leaked information?

2. What is "leak fatigue"?

"WHY WIKILEAKS' 'WAR LOGS' ARE NO PENTAGON PAPERS," BY RICHARD TOFEL, FROM *PROPUBLICA*, JULY 26, 2010

The WikiLeaks documents on the Afghanistan war have brought suggestions such as this one (from *The New York Times*, the newspaper that published both) that they represent "the Pentagon Papers of our time." Not quite. Here are a few quick thoughts on the analogy:

WHAT'S IMPORTANTLY SIMILAR TO THE PENTAGON PAPERS

The greatest similarity between the WikiLeaks trove and the Pentagon Papers is that the documents end before the current administration's policy began. In political terms, that is hugely important.

The Pentagon Papers, of course, were a secret study, commissioned during the Lyndon Johnson administration by Secretary of Defense Robert McNamara. The period under study ended in 1968, and the papers were not made public until 1971. Johnson left office in 1969, and was succeeded by a president of the opposing party, Richard Nixon. Nixon promised a shift in Vietnam policy, and while his policy did not differ as much in practice as he had hinted that it would while campaigning, he was not held responsible, by most voters, for the deepening mess of the Johnson years.

In the current case, as the White House has repeatedly pointed out in the last 18 hours, the papers end before President Barack Obama's announcement last year of an Afghanistan policy that departed from that of President

George W. Bush. (That policy, of course, has centered on significantly increasing the number of troops, and focusing more on counterinsurgency.)

WHAT'S CRUCIALLY DIFFERENT FROM THE PENTAGON PAPERS

In terms of important disclosures, it's not even close, with the historical importance of today's documents likely to be relatively minor, and that of the Pentagon Papers enormous. The most significant revelations today include the Taliban's limited use of heat-seeking missiles (which had been previously reported, though little-noticed), and the Pakistani intelligence service's constant double-dealing and occasional cooperation with the Taliban (long the subject of news stories, and even of some official complaints).

In 1971, in contrast, the Pentagon Papers revealed a host of important discrepancies between the public posture of the U.S. government with respect to Vietnam and the truth -- from the Truman administration, through the times of Presidents Eisenhower, Kennedy and Johnson.

These included Johnson's dissembling during the 1964 presidential campaign and in the run-up to the key decision in 1965 to send large numbers of combat troops, as well as confirmation of U.S. involvement in the 1963 coup against South Vietnamese premier Ngo Dinh Diem. And perhaps most famously, was the evidence that the administration had decided to escalate the war before the 1964 Tonkin Gulf Resolution gave it the authority to do so.

There are many reasons for the differences between these two troves of documents, but perhaps the most important is that today's documents provide a "ground-level" view of the war, while the Pentagon Papers offered a classic "top-down" perspective. Wars are fought on the ground, and the perspective such a view provides can be invaluable. But many of a war's key secrets, especially in political terms, are generated at the top.

THE REAL IMPACT OF THE PENTAGON PAPERS

There is a lot of loose talk today about the impact of the Pentagon Papers. Much of it, I suspect, stems from this in the Wikipedia entry: "The revelations widened the credibility gap between the US government and the people, hurting President Richard Nixon's war effort." In fact, a much stronger argument can be made for the proposition that there was almost no impact on the Nixon administration's ability to conduct the war as it wished. Nixon's policy continued apace, through the peace negotiations of 1972 (during a presidential campaign!), continuing with the Christmas 1972 bombing of Hanoi and Haiphong harbor, and including the January 1973 peace accords.

The great antiwar demonstrations that many of us recall -- the March on Washington, the student Moratorium, Kent State -- all took place before the publication of the papers. Nixon invaded Cambodia 14 months earlier. What happened after the papers was that Nixon coasted to re-election by one of the largest majorities in American history, and his adviser Henry Kissinger won a share of the Nobel Peace Prize for "ending" the Vietnam War.

That said, there were profound effects from the release of the Pentagon Papers. They came in how the Nixon administration responded to the leak and the publication of the papers. First, the administration went to court and soon suffered, in the Supreme Court, the most significant defeat for the executive branch in the national security field since Lincoln's suspension of *habeas corpus* was struck down in 1866 (i.e. after the Civil War ended and after Lincoln was killed).

Beyond the legal battle, Nixon and his henchmen launched the "plumbers" operation (to stem more leaks) and thus set off down the road that led to Watergate -- and all that followed. These became the central American political events of the 1970s, and hugely weakened the presidency, with consequences including the Gerald Ford administration's powerlessness with Congress when the North Vietnamese violated the peace accords in 1975.

How the Obama administration will react today is, of course, still emerging, and already being debated. But where Nixon brought suit and ordered burglaries, I find an early sign in this from the *New York Times* Washington bureau chief, Dean Baquet:

> "I did in fact go the White House and lay out for them what we had," Baquet said. "We did it to give them the opportunity to comment and react. They did. They also praised us for the way we handled it, for giving them a chance to discuss it, and for handling the information with care. And for being responsible."

1. What are the differences between the Panama Papers and the Pentagon Papers?

2. How did the Pentagon Papers lead to Watergate?

"WIKILEAKS, THE CIA AND THE SAD REALITY OF THE WORLD," BY ENRIQUE DANS, FROM ENRIQUE DANS AT MEDIUM.COM, MARCH 8, 2017

The release by WikiLeaks of Vault 7, a file with more than eight thousand documents detailing some of the techniques that the CIA uses to access information on iOS or Android devices, on our computers, as well as the use of smart TVs to listen to conversations and other equally chilling practices is undoubtedly worrying and revives tensions between technology companies and government spy agencies… but it is hardly surprising.

In reality, it is simply further evidence that spy agencies adapt to the surrounding ecosystem which now consists of devices permanently connected through networks. Today's "spy kit" no longer consists of a magnifying glass, a flashlight, a pistol or a fake beard, but a computer and an internet connection.

The role of a government espionage agency is to spy. That this espionage is carried out to guarantee the security of a nation or to preserve a certain tyrannical regime is another question that depends on the concept of politics, liberties or ethics of the government of each country. In other words, being scandalized because there are spies or because the spies are engaged in spying is at best naive and at worst a sign of idiocy, and wondering why these spies adapt their methods to the times we live is absurd: Given that we are supposed to accept—although no one asked us—that governments have to have spies and that we have to pay for them with our taxpayers' money, would we prefer them to continue using outdated tools and methods? Do you want to fight modern spies with sophisticated online tools from a foreign country with agents equipped with magnifying glasses and fake beards?

Obviously, the answer to that question is a very big "it depends". In the first place, because we would obviously prefer a world without spies. But since that isn't going to happen, we will have to consider the different scenarios. If in a country we understand that spies are used to catch terrorists, drug traffickers, criminals or other threats, we will surely want these spies to have the best tools available, and to possess the expertise to invent any they need. If, on the contrary, we think that spies are used to control us, to detect protests or insurgency, to persecute those who think differently and to ignore our most basic human rights, the idea that these spies have the best tools is deeply worrying. It is not the same to live in a democracy where we expect spies to be able to detect a terrorist cell preparing an attack in the center of the city, as to be a homosexual in an Islamic country, or a pro-human rights activist living in a dictatorship, or a non-believer living in a theocracy.

The only thing that the latest WikiLeaks revelations show is that the world is as complex as it was twenty years ago, or probably even more. Twenty years ago government agencies were eavesdropping on our phones and our conversations with microphones, by reading our lips, our letters or tracking our trips: now they tap into our connected electronic devices, which will soon be all devices. As much as we may be concerned or outraged, this is the reality of our world. Things have moved on since the Cold War, and as technology companies strive to use ever more advanced technologies to protect their users, spies will, in turn, find more and better techniques to keep spying on them. Like it or not, spies gonna spy.

Are these leaks good or evil? On the one hand, they lead us to a more transparent society, to understand much better what happens to our privacy and to our data, to put pressure on both the spies and the tech companies (thus leading to further innovation), and to help clarify if there were any wrongdoings (such as spying on innocent citizens without a warrant, as it clearly seems to be the case). On the other hand, they contribute to generate a collective state of psychosis that could collide with our freedom to do ordinary things, and could serve as an example, even a guide, to spies in less developed countries, with all the consequences to citizens in those countries that this possibility may entail. The leaks are not good or evil: they just happen. But if you ask me, I rather live in a world where WikiLeaks exists and plays a significant role in controlling certain behaviors.

Furthermore, we must appreciate the efforts of technology companies to fix the security holes that have allowed spies to spy, and try to be pragmatic and, above all, see things in perspective: most of us, average Joes or Janes who live in democracies, are probably not spied on. What's more, despite of what was being implied or said yesterday, the CIA has not been able to crack Signal's encryption, nor WhatsApp's, or Telegram's, nor many others. Instead, what they have found are methods to access the devices that originate or receive messages, which can allow them to read those messages at the point of origin or destination. So we don't yet have to delete apps we thought were safe, and besides, most of us are using them for things that are of no interest whatsoever for the spies of our governments. If you are being spied on and haven't done anything wrong, then be worried. But not about the spies… about your government! As ever, the problem lies not in technology, but in who uses it and why.

1. Are spies really a necessity?

2. What tools does the modern spy kit consist of?

CHAPTER 2

WHAT THE GOVERNMENT AND POLITICIANS SAY

While many whistleblowers are exposing government secrets, the government also relies on whistleblowers to alert them of citizens' misdeeds. This means the government must encourage and cultivate a culture of ethical whistleblowing, while also protecting themselves from whistleblowers. The United States isn't the only country wondering how to deal with whistleblowers. Canada and Australia are also striving to create strong whistleblower protection laws. Canada found that incentivizing whistleblowers helped raise the number of complaints they received. Fraud cases, like those brought against for-profit schools, show how the government can benefit from whistleblowers. In the case of for-profit schools, whistleblowers were able to prove that schools had defrauded taxpayers out of billions of dollars. The Department of Education and the Consumer Financial Protection Bureau were able to take legal action based on the information gathered from leaks. In this case, whistleblowing had allowed the government to help protect citizens from predatory businesses.

"A LOOPHOLE IN WHISTLEBLOWER PROTECTION WOULD BE CLOSED WITH THE FOLLOW THE RULES ACT," BY JESSE RIFKIN, FROM GOVTRACK.US, JUNE 14, 2017

Imagine you're a federal worker and your boss asks you to violate a federal law that's been passed by Congress. If you refuse to do so—instead pledging fidelity to the law—you're protected from employment retaliation thanks to the Whistleblower Protection Act of 1989. It's your superior who's considered in the wrong for making the illegal request in the first place, not you for disobeying your boss.

But what if you disobey an order to violate a *regulation* instituted by the executive branch instead, rather than a law passed by Congress? The difference may seem minor, but the consequences are major: you're not protected at all.

The Follow the Rules Act, labelled H.R. 657 in the House, was introduced by Rep. Sean Duffy (R-WI7) to correct this discrepancy.

THE CONTEXT

This discrepancy never came up until last year. Timothy Rainey was a State Department employee who was instructed by his boss to make a contractor rehire a previously-fired subcontractor, in violation of an existing federal regulation. Rainey refused, and his boss retaliated by removing his responsibilities as a contracting officer.

Although Rainey would have been protected had he refused to violate a law passed by Congress, he instead refused to violate a rule or regulation instituted by the executive branch and wasn't protected at all. A federal appeals court upheld Rainey's punishment in the precedent-setting decision *Rainey v. Merit Systems Protection Board* in June 2016.

This decision proved especially controversial in the legal community because the appeals court's decision relied upon a Supreme Court precedent in a way that many believed twisted the Supreme Court's original logic, since that Supreme Court decision found in favor of a federal employee rather than against.

WHAT THE BILL DOES AND WHAT SUPPORTERS SAY

The Follow the Rules Act is one page long, and would clarify that a rule or regulation is given the same legal weight as a law when it comes to federal employee protections.

An example provided by a Duffy press release regards a rule or regulation created to sanction North Korea. A federal employee who is told by a superior to violate the North Korea sanctions would currently have no protections if they refuse.

Supporters say the legislation helps ensure effective governance, especially in a highly polarized political environment when Democrats and even some Republicans have heightened concern about political pressure on career civil service employees.

"Given attacks on the federal workforce... we need to do all we can to ensure that federal employees are allowed to perform their jobs free from political pressure to violate laws, rules, and regulations," House cosponsor Rep. Gerry Connolly (D-VA11) said in a press release. "We cannot tolerate the issuance of gag orders to silence dissent. And we cannot permit the firing of agency employees who have differing political views from our own or from Administration actions."

VOTES AND ODDS OF PASSAGE

The legislation passed the House unanimously 407–0 on May 1, after first attracting 11 cosponsors, six Democrats and five Republicans. It then passed the Senate by a unanimous consent voice vote on May 25. Now it goes to President Trump.

A previous version passed the House in November 2016, but never received a Senate vote.

1. What effect would the Follow the Rules Act have?

2. Why are whistleblower protections important for federal employees?

"TWO BILLS CONGRESS IS CONSIDERING MAY CREATE FUTURE EDWARD SNOWDENS," BY GOVTRACK.US, JULY 5, 2016

Edward Snowden shocked the world in 2013 with millions of leaked documents from the National Security Agency (NSA) revealing classified technological capabilities for mass surveillance. Yet because Snowden was a government contractor through the company Booz Allen Hamilton rather than a government employee, whistleblower protections are not available to him.

S. 795, "A bill to enhance whistleblower protection for contractor and grantee employees," would add protections for contractors in almost every area except the intelligence community. It passed the Senate in June. Could another bill introduced by the same senator to protect intelligence contractors like Snowden also pass the Senate too?

WHAT THE BILLS DO

S. 795 would extend existing whistleblower protections to contractors, subcontractors, and grantees. The protections include protection from retaliation by supervisors for reporting violations of the law, abuse of authority, or a danger to public health or safety, according to the Office of Personnel Management. That's of no small importance, with nearly half a million contractors holding "top secret" clearances but not having those protections currently granted to government employees.

However, the bill does not include the intelligence community of which Snowden was a part. Intelligence contractors were stripped of whistleblower protections in 2012—the year before Snowden made his disclosures. Another bill, S. 794, introduced the same day last March as S. 795, would reinstate whistleblower protections for intelligence contractors.

Neither bill appears to be retroactive, meaning that their protections may not apply to Snowden himself—although they would apply to potential future Snowdens, whether in the intelligence community or outside of it. (Fearing government prosecution, Snowden fled to Hong Kong and then to Moscow where he remains to this day, unable to leave due to the U.S. government revoking his passport.)

WHAT SUPPORTERS SAY

Supporters say that the bills would keep government honest and help prevent retaliation against those who are trying to expose the truth.

"Whistleblowers are the taxpayers' best friend," the bills' sponsor Sen. Claire McCaskill (D-MO) said in a press release. "These folks play a critical role in keeping our government accountable to its citizens by exposing waste, fraud and abuse—and we've got to surround them with the robust legal protections that enable them to come forward to report wrongdoing."

Similar legislation introduced by McCaskill in the previous Congress received support from more than 40 groups include the American Civil Liberties Union, Human Rights Watch, and the Sunlight Foundation. "In the absence of adequate protections, they [contractors] have only two alternatives to almost certain retaliation: 1) remain silent observers of wrongdoing; or 2) make anonymous leaks," the open letter said. "Whistleblowers must be free to report abuses of power that betray the public trust without fear. It is imperative that Congress quickly fill this accountability loophole."

WHAT OPPONENTS SAY

Opponents say that protections would only encourage leaks that could endanger national security and undermine an existing sensible hierarchy within the government.

Robert Litt, General Counsel for the Director of National Intelligence, called the creation of contractor whistleblower protections "complicated" because "A contractor isn't working for the government," making it a dubious proposition whether they're worthy of equivalent legal protections as government employees.

Former Rep. Mike Rogers (R-MI), former chair of the House Intelligence Committee and one of Snowden's biggest critics, said there are alternate better avenues already in existence for would-be whistleblowers. "There are already strong protections in place for true whistle blowers—they can take their concerns to a variety of inspectors general and ombudsmen throughout the Intelligence Community, and they can talk to the House and Senate Intelligence Committees. I have seen many people take advantage of these channels, which allow a whistleblower to voice concerns about legitimate government abuse in a secure environment," Rogers said.

WHY IT PASSED AND ODDS OF PASSAGE

Introduced last March by McCaskill, the S. 795 bill for civilian and defense (but not intelligence) contractors received a floor vote last month. The Senate Home-land Security and Governmental Affairs Committee had approved it by voice vote in February and the full Senate approved it by unanimous consent, both methods under which individual senators' votes aren't recorded. So the public doesn't know whether it passed by a hair or by a landslide.

However, last year's NSA and surveillance reform legislation may be a guide. It passed 338 to 88, nearly the opposite margin of the 315–97 vote back in 2010 to reauthorize most of the Patriot Act, which authorized the existing surveillance methods. Most of that shift was attributed to Snowden and the information he revealed in 2013.

Yet despite that sea change, Congress does not appear to be willing to grant intelligence contractors whistleblower protections just yet. S. 794 has not even received a vote in committee, let alone the entire Senate, and has attracted zero cosponsors.

1. What are the arguments for strong whistleblower protections?

2. What are the arguments against strong whistleblower protections?

"WHO'S REGULATING FOR-PROFIT SCHOOLS? EXECS FROM FOR-PROFIT COLLEGES," BY ANNIE WALDMAN, FROM *PROPUBLICA*, FEBRUARY 26, 2016

College accreditors have come under scrutiny recently for allowing for-profit schools to collect billions in federal aid despite low graduation and high default rates.

Accreditors are supposed to be watchdogs for college quality. They are not government agencies but colleges need an accreditor's seal of approval so students can qualify for federal loans.

The agency that has received the most heat is the Accrediting Council for Independent Colleges and Schools. ACICS allowed Corinthian Colleges Inc. to keep on operating right up until the for-profit college chain collapsed after evidence emerged that the schools had lured thousands of poor students into predatory loans. The accreditor placed a Corinthian campus on its "honor roll" just months before the Education Department forced the school to shut down.

ACICS, which oversees hundreds of for-profit colleges, is now the target of two government investigations. A ProPublica analysis also found that schools overseen by ACICS had the lowest graduation rates compared with other accreditors.

So who are the people behind the beleaguered accreditor? They include executives from some of the most scandal-plagued schools in the country.

We looked at all ACICS commissioners since 2010 and found that two-thirds of them have worked as executives at for-profit schools while sitting on the council. A third of the commissioners came from schools that have been facing consumer-protection lawsuits, investigations by state attorneys general, or federal financial monitoring.

Consider Beth Wilson. Wilson, the executive vice president of Corinthian Colleges, joined ACICS in 2014, less than three months after the California attorney general had filed a lawsuit against Corinthian for deceptive advertising and falsifying placement numbers. Wilson was no stranger to accreditation, as she had previously been the chair of another accreditor of primarily for-profit schools. And she was also no stranger to Corinthian's problems. According to the attorney general's ongoing suit, Wilson ordered employees to alter Corinthian's job-placement statistics.

Wilson did not respond to requests for comment.

Having the majority of commissioners be industry executives violates no federal rules. The Department of Education only requires a small fraction of commissioners to be from outside the industry, and accrediting agencies of both nonprofit and for-profit schools are largely composed of industry players.

However, some education experts argue that potential conflicts of interest in for-profit accreditation are especially troubling because of the heightened scrutiny within the industry.

Robert Shireman, a former deputy undersecretary with the Department of Education and currently a senior fellow at the Century Foundation, calls the accreditation process "a giant cesspool of corruption." Shireman, who has long worked to bolster regulation of for-profit colleges, said the accreditation process "needs to be independent" and not overseen by the industry itself. "It would be like getting the CEOs of the airlines together to review whether the airplanes are safe," he said.

"The scandals surrounding the for-profit college industry have thrown a spotlight on flaws in the accreditation system," said Stephen Burd, senior policy analyst at New America, a nonpartisan think tank. "These agencies turn a blind eye to abuses, and lobby on behalf of the industry."

ACICS' 15 commissioners, who are all unpaid, are the ultimate decision-makers about whether a school receives accreditation. ACICS, like other accrediting agencies, is funded through membership fees from the colleges it oversees, and its commissioners are mainly peer reviewers from member schools.

Al Gray, the executive director of ACICS, said the agency has a strict conflict-of-interest policy and recusal practices that do not allow commissioners to sit in on hearings that involve their own schools.

"It might appear that it's compromised by the fact that the peer reviewers are affiliated with the institutions," said Gray. "But while that may be an appearance, proper protections are put in place in the system to ensure that doesn't occur."

Here is a rundown of a handful of commissioners, their day jobs, and what their schools have been accused of:

COMMISSIONERS DAVID LUCE AND BETH WILSON

When they served: Luce from 2008–2013 (his second term) and Wilson in 2014

Where they also worked: Corinthian Colleges, Inc. Luce was assistant vice president of accreditation and licensing; Wilson was executive vice president.

What their school was getting heat for: A whole lot, including deceptive marketing techniques and predatory loan practices. The list includes investigations from the Government Accountability Office, more than twenty state attorneys general, the Department of Education's inspector general, the Consumer Financial Protection Bureau, and the Securities and Exchange Commission. The Government Accountability Office investigation resulted in a congressional hearing and the Consumer Financial Protection Bureau secured a default judgment finding Corinthian liable for over half a billion dollars. Many of the other investigations are ongoing.

What happened to their school's accreditation: Not much. In the years leading up to its collapse, the number of campuses that ACICS accredited increased from 35 in 2005 to 57 in 2013. By the time the Education Department finalized a deal with Corinthian to close and sell its campuses, ACICS was the school's leading accreditor. In 2014, just months before the department took action, ACICS put a Corinthian campus on its honor roll. ACICS did not revoke the accreditation of any of Corinthian's campuses before the department stepped in.

How much federal aid their school received: Around $1.4 billion annually.

What they say: David Luce and Beth Wilson did not respond to requests for comment. Luce left ACICS' council at the end of his term and Wilson resigned in mid–2014, according to ACICS officials.

COMMISSIONERS JOHN EULIANO AND RICHARD BENNETT

When they served: Euliano from 2011-current and Bennett started this January

Where they also worked: Southern Technical College. Euliano is the founder; Bennett is senior vice president of financial aid.

What their school was getting heat for: Accepting invalid high school diplomas and financial compliance. *The Miami Herald* reported last year that Southern Technical College and others had enrolled students without proof that they finished high school. Two Southern Technical College campuses have also been flagged by the Department of Education for issues of financial responsibility as of December 2015. One campus received the government's lowest possible financial rating for the 2012 school year (the most recent data), a score shared by only 40 of 3,400 colleges across the country. From 2011 to 2012, the college was subject to a Department of Education review to confirm that the school met Federal Student Aid requirements. In a review of two years of data, the department found over $200,000 in liabilities because of compliance issues, including incorrect financial-aid calculations and invalid high-school diplomas.

What happened to their school's accreditation: Again, not much. None of the college's campuses have had their accreditation suspended or revoked. And in 2012 three of the college's campuses were put on the accrediting agency's "honor roll."

How much federal aid their school received: $36 million during the 2013 school year.

What they say: Euliano told ProPublica in an email that there is no conflict of interest within ACICS' council. "Any insinuation that there is any 'home cooking' or that our peer review process is somehow 'the fox running the hen house' (it seems like that is where you are going) is absolutely 100% false," he said. (Read his email.) Euliano also described the department review as "not out of the ordinary" and the liabilities that were found "small compared to the amount of aid processed." Euliano sold the college in 2012, staying on for a year to help with the transition. Bennett said in an email that the low financial score was a result of the sale and that it wasn't a good indicator of the company's fiscal viability. He also said that landing on the department's list of schools with financial-compliance issues is "not always representative of any wrongdoing/ findings from the department." The Department of Education has described the list as a "caution light."

COMMISSIONER FRANCIS GIGLIO

When he served: 2009–2012

Where he also worked: Lincoln Educational Services. Giglio is vice president of compliance and regulatory services.

What his school was getting heat for: The New York attorney general opened an investigation into Lincoln Educational Services in 2011, to see whether the school misrepresented the quality of its education, tuition costs, program accreditation, and its ability to find jobs for students.

What happened to his school's accreditation: Yet again, nothing really: None of the college's campuses have had their accreditation suspended or revoked.

How much federal aid his school received: $200 million during the 2013 school year.

What he says: "If, in fact, in that institution there was some type of conviction or determination that there was fraud, waste or abuse, then that person would no longer be on the commission," Giglio told ProPublica. "But in the meantime, there's always the opportunity for that person to say, This is fiction, these students have said these things, but this isn't truly what's happening." Giglio said that his company has not heard from the attorney general since the college sent in the requested documents. The attorney general's office declined to comment.

COMMISSIONER JEANNE HERRMANN

When she served: 2009–2015

Where she also worked: Globe University/Minnesota School of Business. Herrmann is chief operating officer.

What her school was getting heat for: Job-placement numbers and marketing tactics. In 2013, a former Globe University dean won a whistleblower lawsuit against the school. The dean said she had been fired after complaining about fraudulent job-placement numbers and misleading recruiting practices. The Minnesota attorney general filed a lawsuit against the school in 2014, accusing the colleges of misrepresenting job opportunities to students. That suit is ongoing.

What happened to her school's accreditation: Not much. None of the college's campuses have had their accreditation suspended or revoked.

How much federal aid did her school received: $74 million during the 2013 school year.

What she says: Jeanne Herrmann did not respond to request for comment.

Commissioner Gary Carlson and Edwin Colon

When they served: 2006–2011 and 2009–2014

Where they also worked: ITT Technical Institute. Carlson was vice president of academic affairs at ITT until his retirement in late 2010. Colon was director at an ITT Technical Institute Campus until May 2014, according to his online résumé.

What their school was getting heat for: Job placements and recruiting practices. An ongoing whistleblower lawsuit, brought in 2007, alleges that the school submitted false claims to the government to receive more financial aid. In 2010, a U.S. Senate committee began an investigation into ITT, eventually finding that the company used aggressive recruiting tactics and that many of its students left without finishing their degrees. The Consumer Financial Protection Bureau also opened an investigation in 2013. It filed suit a few months later, accusing the company of predatory lending. In 2014, ITT was hit with a dozen investigations by state attorneys general. The suits from the Consumer Financial Protection Bureau and the attorneys general are ongoing, according to the company's most recent SEC filings.

What happened to their school's accreditation: And again … not much. ACICS has not revoked or suspended any of the college's campuses.

How much federal aid their school received: $796 million during the 2013 school year alone.

What they say: "I don't think that everybody that's under investigation is always immediately guilty," said Gary Carlson. "When we paintbrush one whole industry as being bad because of some not following the rules, it's probably a mistake." Edwin Colon did not respond to request for comment.

In response to the list of commissioners from scrutinized schools, Anthony Bieda, vice president for external affairs at ACICS, described the council as "highly ethical" and "committed public servants who receive no pay for their service." Bieda said the commissioners were either nominated or appointed before the scrutiny of their companies occurred.

"If issues related to the commissioners' institution were raised in a council meeting, the commissioners always and diligently recuse themselves from the discussion and any subsequent decision," said Bieda. He added that "the commissioners themselves were not under scrutiny or accused of wrongdoing."

Ultimately, the makeup of the accreditation boards reflects the industry itself, warts and all.

"The way the agency commissioners are selected, it stands to reason that an agency that covers what we'll call at risk schools will have commissioners from at-risk places," said Susan Phillips, the chair of a Department of Education committee that reviews accreditors.

1. Was it ethical for whistleblowers to make the corruption in the for-profit school accreditation process known?

2. What kind of issues did for-profit school whistleblowers bring to light?

"18 U.S. CODE § 798 - DISCLOSURE OF CLASSIFIED INFORMATION," FROM THE US GOVERNMENT PUBLISHING OFFICE, JANUARY 3, 2012

(a) Whoever knowingly and willfully communicates, furnishes, transmits, or otherwise makes available to an unauthorized person, or publishes, or uses in any manner prejudicial to the safety or interest of the United States or for the benefit of any foreign government to the detriment of the United States any classified information—

(1) concerning the nature, preparation, or use of any code, cipher, or cryptographic system of the United States or any foreign government; or

(2) concerning the design, construction, use, maintenance, or repair of any device, apparatus, or appliance used or prepared or planned for use by the United States or any foreign government for cryptographic or communication intelligence purposes; or

(3) concerning the communication intelligence activities of the United States or any foreign government; or

(4) obtained by the processes of communication intelligence from the communications of any foreign government, knowing the same to have been obtained by such processes—

Shall be fined under this title or imprisoned not more than ten years, or both.

(b) As used in subsection (a) of this section—

The term "classified information" means information which, at the time of a violation of this section, is, for reasons of national security, specifically designated by a United States Government Agency for limited or restricted dissemination or distribution;

The terms "code," "cipher," and "cryptographic system" include in their meanings, in addition to their usual meanings, any method of secret writing and any mechanical or electrical device or method used for the purpose of disguising or concealing the contents, significance, or meanings of communications;

The term "foreign government" includes in its meaning any person or persons acting or purporting to act for or on behalf of any faction, party, department, agency, bureau, or military force of or within a foreign country, or for or on behalf of any government or any person or persons purporting to act as a government within a foreign country, whether or not such government is recognized by the United States;

The term "communication intelligence" means all procedures and methods used in the interception of communications and the obtaining of information from such communications by other than the intended recipients;

The term "unauthorized person" means any person who, or agency which, is not authorized to receive information of the categories set forth in subsection (a) of this section, by the President, or by the head of a department or agency of the United States Government which is expressly designated by the President to engage in communication intelligence activities for the United States.

(c) Nothing in this section shall prohibit the furnishing, upon lawful demand, of information to any regularly constituted committee of the Senate or House of Representatives of the United States of America, or joint committee thereof.

(d)(1) Any person convicted of a violation of this section shall forfeit to the United States irrespective of any provision of State law—

(A) any property constituting, or derived from, any proceeds the person obtained, directly or indirectly, as the result of such violation; and

(B) any of the person's property used, or intended to be used, in any manner or part, to commit, or to facilitate the commission of, such violation.

(2) The court, in imposing sentence on a defendant for a conviction of a violation of this section, shall order that the defendant forfeit to the United States all property described in paragraph (1).

(3) Except as provided in paragraph (4), the provisions of subsections (b), (c), and (e) through (p) of section 413 of the Comprehensive Drug Abuse Prevention and Control Act of 1970 (21 U.S.C. 853(b), (c), and (e)–(p)), shall apply to—

(A) property subject to forfeiture under this subsection;

(B) any seizure or disposition of such property; and

(C) any administrative or judicial proceeding in relation to such property,

if not inconsistent with this subsection.

(4) Notwithstanding section 524(c) of title 28, there shall be deposited in the Crime Victims Fund established under section 1402 of the Victims of Crime Act of 1984 (42 U.S.C. 10601) [1] all amounts from the forfeiture of property under this subsection remaining after the payment of expenses for forfeiture and sale authorized by law.

(5) As used in this subsection, the term "State" means any State of the United States, the District of Columbia, the Commonwealth of Puerto Rico, and any territory or possession of the United States.

1. What kind of activity does this law ban?

"CANADA OFFERS AUSTRALIA A BLUEPRINT FOR PROTECTING AND MOTIVATING CORPORATE WHISTLEBLOWERS," BY JANET AUSTIN, FROM *THE CONVERSATION*, JULY 2, 2017

As the Australian government considers how to incentivize and protect corporate whistleblowers, it could look to Canada's system. The securities regulator for Canada's largest and most populous province, the Ontario Securities Commission, launched its whistleblower program last year.

The program is accompanied by some important changes in law to protect whistleblowers from retaliation, but also a bounty to motivate employees to inform authorities of any wrongdoing. Both of these are sorely lacking in Australia's corporate environment.

The Canadian changes were inspired, at least to some extent, by the whistleblower provisions introduced in the US as a result of the Dodd-Frank Wall Street Reform and Consumer Protection Act 2010. However, while

Ontario did embrace some of these changes, there are some notable differences.

For a start, any provisions in an employment agreement that prevents employees from whistleblowing are now void, thanks to changes to the Ontario Securities Act. Any reprisal action employers take against whistleblowers is now also an offence.

The Dodd Frank Act had introduced similar provisions and provided a right for whistleblowers to sue their employer if they'd retaliated against them. The Ontario government is considering introducing legislation to grant whistleblowers a similar right.

In Australia, similar legislation to protect whistleblowers from reprisals is unlikely to be controversial. However, the introduction of a financial award or bounty system would be more contentious. Lawyers acting for businesses argue that it undermines internal compliance and can end up rewarding those who are complicit in the illegal behavior.

Despite these claims, Ontario did decide to introduce a financial award for reporting breaches of Ontario securities law to the Ontario Securities Commission. The point of the program is not to compensate whistleblowers for losses they may suffer, but to motivate them to come forward with high quality information. This information would otherwise be difficult to obtain, so it helps regulators increase the number and efficiency of investigations.

The regulators also hope the threat of being reported for misconduct will motivate companies to improve internal whistleblower reporting systems and to deal more proactively with illegal behavior. This approach works with the Ontario Securities Commission's credit for cooperation program, where companies that self-report violations early are dealt with more leniently than those reported by a whistleblower.

Unlike the whistleblower bounty program in the US which is paid for and administered by the Securities and Exchange Commission, the Ontario Securities Commission award program is designed to be self-funding. Because of this, the awards in Canada are likely to be lower, usually between 5% and 15% of the total sanctions imposed where these amounts total CAD$1 million or more. Under the Securities and Exchange Commission's program, the award is set at between 10% and 30%.

Also unlike the Securities and Exchange Commission's program, awards made under the Ontario Securities Commission's program are capped at a maximum of CAD$1.5 million, irrespective of whether or not the Commission collects the sanctions. But this can increase to a maximum of CAD$5 million if sanctions of over CAD$10 million are actually collected.

The Ontario system illustrates that it's possible to design a cost effective system, with lower awards than in the US, to drive improvements in companies' responses to reports of illegal behavior. In fact, Heidi Franken, chief of the Ontario Securities Commission's Office of the Whistleblower, reported that since the launch of their program the Office has received a significant increase in persons coming forward with valuable information.

To be effective, however, any system Australia implements should contain a real prospect of significant penalties, so that at least some whistleblowers will receive an award.

In Ontario, the Ontario Securities Commission can ensure whistleblowers are paid because it has a broad power to seek disgorgement of profits and administrative penalties of up to CAD$1 million for each breach. It does so via proceedings held before an administrative tribunal, comprised of Commissioners from the Ontario Securities Commission.

The Ontario Securities Commission is usually successful in these proceedings and penalties are only overturned infrequently on appeal. This is because courts give a high degree of deference to the decisions of this specialized administrative tribunal.

Australia's regulator, the Australian Securities and Investments Commission (ASIC), doesn't have a similar power and ASIC's current powers to obtain civil penalties are weak in comparison.

So for a whistleblowing award program to work in Australia, the federal government may need to enhance ASIC's powers or find an alternative source of funds to pay whistleblower bounties.

1. What are some of the methods Canada uses to encourage whistleblowers?

2. How do whistleblower bounties affect whistleblowing trends?

EXCERPT FROM "YOUR RIGHTS AS A WHISTLEBLOWER," BY THE OCCUPATIONAL SAFETY AND HEALTH ADMINISTRATION (OSHA), US DEPARTMENT OF LABOR

You may file a complaint with OSHA if your employer retaliates against you by taking unfavorable personnel action because you engaged in protected activity relating to workplace safety or health, asbestos in schools, cargo containers, airline, commercial motor carrier, consumer product, environmental, financial reform, food safety, health insurance reform, motor vehicle safety, nuclear, pipeline, public transportation agency, railroad, maritime, motor vehicle safety, and securities laws.

UNFAVORABLE PERSONNEL ACTIONS

Your employer may be found to have retaliated against you if your protected activity was a contributing or motivating factor in its decision to take unfavorable personnel action against you.

Such actions may include:

- Applying or issuing a policy which provides for an unfavorable personnel action due to activity protected by a whistleblower law enforced by OSHA
- Blacklisting
- Demoting
- Denying overtime or promotion
- Disciplining
- Denying benefits
- Failing to hire or rehire
- Firing or laying off

- Intimidation
- Making threats
- Reassignment to a less desirable position, including one adversely affecting prospects for promotion
- Reducing pay or hours
- Suspension

FILING A COMPLAINT

If you believe that your employer retaliated against you because you exercised your legal rights as an employee, contact OSHA as soon as possible because you must file your complaint within the legal time limits.

An employee can file a complaint with OSHA by visiting or calling the local OSHA office or sending a written complaint to the closest OSHA regional or area office. Written complaints may be filed by facsimile, electronic communication, hand delivery during business hours, U.S. mail (confirmation services recommended), or other third-party commercial carrier. The date of the postmark, facsimile, electronic communication, telephone call, hand delivery, delivery to a third-party commercial carrier, or in-person filing at an OSHA office is considered the date filed. No particular form is required and complaints may be submitted in any language.

For OSHA area office contact information, please call 1-800-321-OSHA (6742) or visit www.osha.gov/html /RAmap.html.

Upon receipt of a complaint, OSHA will first review it to determine whether it is valid on its face. All complaints are investigated in accord with the statutory requirements. With the exception of employees of the U.S. Postal Service, public sector employees (those employed as municipal, county, state, territorial or federal workers) are not covered by the *Occupational Safety and Health Act* (OSH Act). Non-federal public sector employees and, except in Connecticut, New York, New Jersey, the Virgin Islands, and Illinois, private sector employees are covered in states which operate their own occupational safety and health programs approved by Federal OSHA. For information on the 27 State Plan states, call 1-800-321-OSHA (6742), or visit www.osha.gov/dcsp/osp/index.html.

A federal employee who wishes to file a complaint alleging retaliation due to disclosure of a substantial and specific danger to public health or safety or involving occupational safety or health should contact the Office of Special Counsel (www.osc.gov) and OSHA's Office of Federal Agency Programs (www.osha.gov/dep/enforce-ment/dep_offices.html).

Coverage of public sector employees under the other statutes administered by OSHA varies by statute. If you are a public sector employee and you are unsure whether you are covered under a whistleblower protec-tion statute, call 1-800-321-OSHA (6742) for assistance, or visit www.whistleblowers.gov.

HOW OSHA DETERMINES WHETHER RETALIATION TOOK PLACE

The investigation must reveal that:
- The employee engaged in protected activity;
- The employer knew about or suspected the protected activity;
- The employer took an adverse action; and
- The protected activity motivated or contributed to the adverse action.

If the evidence supports the employee's allegation and a settlement cannot be reached, OSHA will generally issue an order, which the employer may contest, requiring the employer to reinstate the employee, pay back wages, restore benefits, and other possible remedies to make the employee whole. Under some of the statutes the employer must comply with the reinstatement order immediately. In cases under the *Occupational Safety and Health Act*, *Asbestos Hazard Emergency Response Act*, and the *International Safe Container Act*, the Secretary of Labor will file suit in federal district court to obtain relief.

Partial List of Whistleblower Protections

WHISTLEBLOWER PROTECTIONS UNDER THE OSH ACT

The OSH Act protects workers who complain to their employer, OSHA or other government agencies about unsafe or unhealthful working conditions in the workplace or environmental problems. You cannot be transferred, denied a raise, have your hours reduced, be fired, or punished in any other way because you used any right given to you under the OSH Act. Help is available from OSHA for whistleblowers.

If you have been punished or discriminated against for using your rights, you must file a complaint with OSHA within 30 days of the alleged reprisal for most complaints. No form is required, but you must send a letter or call the OSHA Area Office nearest you to report the discrimination (within 30 days of the alleged discrimination).

You have a limited right under the OSH Act to refuse to do a job because conditions are hazardous. You may do so under the OSH Act only when (1) you believe that you face death or serious injury (and the situation is so clearly hazardous that any reasonable person would believe the same thing); (2) you have tried, where possible, to get your employer to correct the condition, and been unable to obtain a correction and there is no other way to do the job safely; and (3) the situation is so urgent that you do not have time to eliminate the hazard through regulatory channels such as calling OSHA. For details, see www.osha.gov/as/opa/worker/refuse.html. OSHA cannot enforce union contracts or state laws that give employees the right to refuse to work.

WHISTLEBLOWER PROTECTIONS IN THE TRANSPORTATION INDUSTRY

Employees whose jobs directly affect commercial motor vehicle safety or security are protected from retaliation by their employers for, among other things, reporting violations of federal or state commercial motor carrier safety or security regulations, or refusing to operate a vehicle because of violations of federal commercial motor vehicle safety or security regulations or because they have a reasonable apprehension of death or serious injury to themselves or the public and they have sought from the employer and been unable to obtain correction of the hazardous condition.

Similarly, employees of air carriers, their contractors or subcontractors who raise safety concerns or report violations of FAA rules and regulations are protected from retaliation, as are employees of owners and operators of pipelines, their contractors and subcontractors who report violations of pipeline safety rules and regulations. Employees involved in international shipping who report unsafe shipping containers are also protected. In addition, employees of railroad carriers or public transportation agencies, their contractors or subcontractors who report safety or security conditions or violations of federal rules and regulations relating to railroad or public transportation safety or security are protected from retaliation.

WHISTLEBLOWER PROTECTIONS FOR VOICING ENVIRONMENTAL CONCERNS

A number of laws protect employees from retaliation because they report violations of environmental laws related to drinking water and water pollution, toxic substances, solid waste disposal, air quality and air pollution, asbestos in schools, and hazardous waste disposal sites. The Energy Reorganization Act protects employees from retaliation for raising safety concerns in the nuclear power industry and in nuclear medicine.

WHISTLEBLOWER PROTECTIONS WHEN REPORTING CORPORATE FRAUD

Employees who work for publicly traded companies or companies required to file certain reports with the Securities and Exchange Commission are protected from retaliation for reporting alleged mail, wire, bank or securities fraud; violations of SEC rules or regulations of the SEC; or violations of federal laws relating to fraud against shareholders.

WHISTLEBLOWER PROTECTIONS FOR VOICING CONSUMER PRODUCT CONCERNS

Employees of consumer product manufacturers, importers, distributors, retailers, and private labelers are protected from retaliation for reporting reasonably perceived violations of any statute or regulation within the jurisdiction of the Consumer Safety Product Safety Commission.

MORE INFORMATION

To obtain more information on whistleblower laws, go to www.whistleblowers.gov.

1. What rights and protections does OSHA grant whistleblowers?

CHAPTER 3

WHAT THE COURTS SAY

The courts have two jobs when it comes to dealing with whistleblowers: protecting those who expose illegal activities from retaliation and punishing those who expose information with the intent to harm others. The Espionage Act makes it illegal for individuals to knowingly share classified information with the intent to harm the United States. Proving malicious intent can be difficult especially in cases like that of Private Chelsea Manning, who leaked information which could potentially harm military operations but also exposed the true extent of civilian casualties in the Iraq and Afghan wars. While the court did find Manning guilty on twenty-two counts, she was acquitted on charges of "aiding the enemy." President Barack Obama later commuted her sentence. The courts are also responsible for holding the executive and legislative branches of government accountable to the laws. Whistleblowers, like Manning, can expose government corruption that may not have come to light any other way.

"WATCH OUT, WHISTLEBLOWERS: CONGRESS AND COURTS MOVE TO CURTAIL LEAKS," BY MARIAN WANG, FROM *PROPUBLICA*, MAY 12, 2011

House Republicans introduced legislation yesterday targeting the already-delayed whistleblower rule in the Dodd-Frank financial reform law. The proposed change would require corporate whistleblowers to report problems internally before going to financial regulators. The move, backed by the U.S. Chamber of Commerce, is just the latest in a series of setbacks for those who favor strengthening whistleblower rules to encourage reporting of wrongdoing within government and businesses.

Whistleblowers were dealt another blow last week when a federal court of appeals ruled that corporate whistleblower protections don't cover leaks to the media. According to the *Los Angeles Times*, the panel of judges ruled that individuals blowing the whistle on publicly traded companies are protected from retaliation only when they report the wrongdoing to financial regulators—which could discourage future leaks to the media.

Whistleblower groups are also protesting a provision in the Intelligence Authorization Bill that would allow intelligence officials to penalize employees and former employees for disclosure of classified information without needing a conviction to do so. The Government Accountability Project has said that under the proposed law, intelligence officials need only reach a "determination" that a knowing violation occurred.

The Obama administration has also been cracking down on major breaches of classified government information and is working to build a case against WikiLeaks founder Julian Assange. NPR reports that the effort is part of a broader campaign by the Obama administration to curtail leaks:

> National security experts say they can't remember a time when the Justice Department has pursued so many criminal cases based on leaks of government secrets. Steve Aftergood of the Federation of American Scientists has been following five separate prosecutions, part of what he calls a tremendous surge by the Obama administration.

And according to a rather ironic report this week by the U.K.'s New Statesman, Assange himself has been trying to prevent leaks within WikiLeaks by making his own associates sign confidentiality agreements and imposing a nearly $20 million penalty for anyone who leaks the organization's leaked material. If it works, this type of agreement could delay the disclosure of some of the confidential documents that have proved useful in reporting on the Middle East revolutions and other international affairs. WikiLeaks, after all, has been known to tout material in its possession while sitting on its release.

1. Should whistleblower protections cover leaks to the media?

2. Should whistleblowers have to report issues internally before going to the media in order to be protected from retaliation?

"CLAIM ON "ATTACKS THWARTED" BY NSA SPREADS DESPITE LACK OF EVIDENCE," BY JUSTIN ELLIOTT AND THEODORIC MEYER, FROM *PROPUBLICA*, OCT 23, 2013

THE AGENCY, PRESIDENT OBAMA, AND MEMBERS OF CONGRESS HAVE ALL SAID NSA SPYING PROGRAMS HAVE THWARTED MORE THAN 50 TERRORIST PLOTS. BUT THERE'S NO EVIDENCE THE CLAIM IS TRUE.

UPDATE Dec. 17, 2013: In a new ruling that calls the NSA's phone metadata surveillance likely unconstitutional, U.S. District Court Judge Richard Leon cited this article in his assessment of the agency's claims about thwarted terrorist attacks. [...]

Two weeks after Edward Snowden's first revelations about sweeping government surveillance, President Obama shot back. "We know of at least 50 threats that have been averted because of this information not just in the United States, but, in some cases, threats here in Germany," Obama said during a visit to Berlin in June. "So lives have been saved."

In the months since, intelligence officials, media outlets, and members of Congress from both parties all repeated versions of the claim that NSA surveillance has stopped more than 50 terrorist attacks. The figure has become a key talking point in the debate around the spying programs.

"Fifty-four times this and the other program stopped and thwarted terrorist attacks both here and in Europe — saving real lives," Rep. Mike Rogers, a Michigan Republican who chairs the House Intelligence Committee, said on the House floor in July, referring to programs authorized by a pair of post-9/11 laws. "This isn't a game. This is real."

But there's no evidence that the oft-cited figure is accurate.

The NSA itself has been inconsistent on how many plots it has helped prevent and what role the surveillance programs played. The agency has often made hedged statements that avoid any sweeping assertions about attacks thwarted.

A chart declassified by the agency in July, for example, says that intelligence from the programs on 54 occasions "has contributed to the [U.S. government's] understanding of terrorism activities and, in many cases, has enabled the disruption of potential terrorist events at home and abroad" — a much different claim than asserting that the programs have been responsible for thwarting 54 attacks.

NSA officials have mostly repeated versions of this wording.

When NSA chief Gen. Keith Alexander spoke at a Las Vegas security conference in July, for instance, he referred to "54 different terrorist-related activities," 42 of which were plots and 12 of which were cases in which individuals provided "material support" to terrorism.

But the NSA has not always been so careful.

During Alexander's speech in Las Vegas, a slide in an accompanying slideshow read simply "54 ATTACKS THWARTED."

And in a recent letter to NSA employees, Alexander and John Inglis, the NSA's deputy director, wrote that the agency has "contributed to keeping the U.S. and its allies safe from 54 terrorist plots." (The letter was obtained by reporter Kevin Gosztola from a source with ties to the intelligence community. The NSA did not respond when asked to authenticate it.)

Asked for clarification of the surveillance programs' record, the NSA declined to comment.

Earlier this month, Sen. Patrick Leahy, D-Vt., pressed Alexander on the issue at a Senate Judiciary Committee hearing.

"Would you agree that the 54 cases that keep getting cited by the administration were not all plots, and of the 54, only 13 had some nexus to the U.S.?" Leahy said at the hearing. "Would you agree with that, yes or no?"

"Yes," Alexander replied, without elaborating.

It's impossible to assess the role NSA surveillance played in the 54 cases because, while the agency has provided a full list to Congress, it remains classified.

Officials have openly discussed only a few of the cases (see below), and the agency has identified only one — involving a San Diego man convicted of sending $8,500 to Somalia to support the militant group Al Shabab — in which NSA surveillance played a dominant role.

The surveillance programs at issue fall into two categories: The collection of metadata on all American phone calls under the Patriot Act, and the snooping of electronic communications targeted at foreigners under a 2007 surveillance law. Alexander has said that surveillance authorized by the latter law provided "the initial tip" in roughly half of the 54 cases. The NSA has not released examples of such cases.

After reading the full classified list, Leahy concluded the NSA's surveillance has some value but still questioned the agency's figures.

"We've heard over and over again the assertion that 54 terrorist plots were thwarted" by the two programs, Leahy told Alexander at the Judiciary Committee hearing this month. "That's plainly wrong, but we still get it in letters to members of Congress, we get it in statements. These weren't all plots and they weren't all thwarted. The American people are getting left with the inaccurate impression of the effectiveness of NSA programs."

The origins of the "54" figure go back to a House Intelligence Committee hearing on June 18, less than two weeks after the *Guardian*'s publication of the first story based on documents leaked by Snowden.

At that hearing, Alexander said, "The information gathered from these programs provided the U.S. government with critical leads to help prevent over 50 potential terrorist events in more than 20 countries around the world." He didn't specify what "events" meant. Pressed by Rep. Jim Himes, D-Conn., Alexander said the NSA would send a more detailed breakdown to the committee.

Speaking in Baltimore the next week, Alexander gave an exact figure: 54 cases "in which these programs contributed to our understanding, and in many cases, helped enable the disruption of terrorist plots in the U.S. and in over 20 countries throughout the world."

But members of Congress have repeatedly ignored the distinctions and hedges.

The websites of the Republicans and Democrats on the House Intelligence Committee include pages titled, "54 Attacks in 20 Countries Thwarted By NSA Collection."

And individual congressmen have frequently cited the figure in debates around NSA surveillance.

- Rep. Lynn Westmoreland, R-Ga., who is also on the House Intelligence Committee, released a statement in July referring to "54 terrorist plots that have been foiled by the NSA programs." Asked about the figure, Westmoreland spokeswoman Leslie Shedd told Pro-Publica that "he was citing declassified information directly from the National Security Agency."
- Rep. Brad Wenstrup, R-Ohio, issued a statement in July saying "the programs in question have thwarted 54 specific plots, many targeting Americans on American soil."
- Rep. Joe Heck, R-Nev., issued his own statement the next day: "The Amash amendment would have eliminated Section 215 of the Patriot Act which we know has thwarted 54 terrorist plots against the US (and counting)." (The amendment, which aimed to bar collection of Americans' phone records, was narrowly defeated in the House.)
- Mike Rogers, the Intelligence Committee chairman who credited the surveillance programs with thwarting 54 attacks on the House floor, repeated the claim to Bob Schieffer on CBS' "Face the Nation" in July. "You just heard what he said, senator," Schieffer said, turning to Sen. Mark Udall, D-Colo., an NSA critic. "Fifty-six terror plots here and abroad have been thwarted by the NSA program. So what's wrong with it, then, if it's managed to stop 56 terrorist attacks? That sounds like a pretty good record."
- Asked about Rogers' remarks, House Intelligence Committee spokeswoman Susan Phalen said in a

statement: "In 54 specific cases provided by the NSA, the programs stopped actual plots or put terrorists in jail before they could effectuate further terrorist plotting. These programs save lives by disrupting attacks. Sometimes the information is found early in the planning, and sometimes very late in the planning. But in all those cases these people intended to kill innocent men and women through the use of terror."

- Rep. James Lankford, R-Okla., went even further in a town hall meeting in August. Responding to a question about the NSA vacuuming up Americans' phone records, he said the program had "been used 54 times to be able to interrupt 54 different terrorist plots here in the United States that had originated from overseas in the past eight years. That's documented."

- The same day, Rep. Jim Langevin, D-R.I., who sits on the Intelligence Committee, defended the NSA at a town hall meeting with constituents in Cranston, R.I. "I know that these programs have been directly effective in thwarting and derailing 54 terrorist attacks," he said.

- Asked about Langevin's comments, spokeswoman Meg Fraser said in an email, "The committee was given information from NSA on August 1 that clearly indicated they considered the programs in question to have been used to help disrupt 54 terrorist events. That is the information the Congressman relied on when characterizing the programs at his town hall."

Wenstrup, Heck and Lankford did not respond to requests for comment.

The claims have also appeared in the media. ABC News, CNN and the *New York Times* have all repeated versions of the claim that more than 50 plots have been thwarted by the programs.

The NSA has publicly identified four of the 54 cases. They are:

- The case of Basaaly Moalin, the San Diego man convicted of sending $8,500 to Somalia to support Al Shabab, the terrorist group that has taken responsibility for the attack on a Kenyan mall last month. The NSA has said its collection of American phone records allowed it to determine that a U.S. phone was in contact with a Shabab figure, which in turn led them to Moalin. NSA critic Sen. Ron Wyden, D-Ore., has argued that the NSA could have gotten a court order to get the phone records in question and that the case does not justify the bulk collection of Americans' phone records.

- The case of Najibullah Zazi, who in 2009 plotted to bomb the New York subway system. The NSA has said that an email it intercepted to an account of a known Al Qaeda figure in Pakistan allowed authorities to identify and ultimately capture Zazi. But an Associated Press examination of the case concluded that, again, the NSA's account of the case did not show the need for the new warrantless powers at issue in the current debate. "Even before the surveillance laws of 2007 and 2008, the FBI had the authority to — and did, regularly — monitor email accounts linked to terrorists," the AP reported.

- A case involving David Coleman Headley, the Chicago man who helped plan the 2008 Mumbai terrorist attack. Intelligence officials have said that NSA surveillance helped thwart a subsequent plot involving Headley to attack a Danish newspaper. A ProPublica examination of that episode concluded that it was a tip from British intelligence, rather than NSA surveillance, that led authorities to Headley.

- A case involving a purported plot to attack the New York Stock Exchange. This convoluted episode involves three Americans, including Khalid Ouazzani of Kansas City, Mo., who pleaded guilty in 2010 to bank fraud, money laundering, and conspiracy to provide material support to Al Qaeda. An FBI official said in June that NSA surveillance helped in the case "to detect a nascent plotting to bomb the New York Stock Exchange." But no one has been charged with crimes related to that or any other planned attack. (Ouazzani was sentenced to 14 years last month.)

- The Kansas City Star reported that one of the men in the case had "pulled together a short report with the kind of public information easily available from Google Earth, tourist maps and brochures" and that his contact in Yemen "tore up the report, 'threw it in the street' and never showed it to anyone."

- Court records also suggest that the men in Yemen that Ouazzani sent over $20,000 to may have been scamming him and spent some of the money on personal expenses.

For more from ProPublica on the NSA, read about the agency's campaign to crack Internet security, a look at the surveillance reforms Obama supported before he was president, and a fact-check on claims about the NSA and Sept. 11.

1. What discrepancies do reporters point out between the ways politicians claim NSA information has been used to foil terrorists and cases that have actually been reported?

2. Should politicians support mass surveillance like that conducted by the NSA when other sources of information gathering produce greater or similar results?

"ORDER 59: PROTECTION AND FAIR INCENTIVES FOR GOVERNMENT WHISTLEBLOWERS," BY PAUL BREMER AND THE COALITION PROVISIONAL AUTHORITY

Pursuant to my authority as Administrator of the Coalition Provisional Authority, under the laws and usages of war, and consistent with relevant U.N. Security Council resolutions, including Resolutions 1483 and 1511 (2003),

Reconfirming the principles set forth in CPA Order Nos. 55, 57, and 77, which established, respectively, the Iraqi Commission on Public Integrity, the Inspectors General for individual ministries, and the Iraqi Board of Supreme Audit,

Avowing to protect the rights of every Iraqi to expose government corruption and wrongdoing by contacting and cooperating with these institutions,

Committed to providing meaningful avenues for the Iraqi people, individually and collectively, to hold government leaders and institutions accountable without fear of repercussion or retribution,

Determined to restore trust and confidence in the honesty and integrity of public officials at all levels of government, and to ensure that public offices in Iraq are truly public trusts of the Iraqi people,

Recognizing that the CPA is committed to the effective administration of Iraq, and that building the Iraqi capacity to fight corruption contributes to civilian administration,

I hereby promulgate the following:

SECTION 1

PURPOSE

This Order promotes active enforcement of anti-corruption laws by encouraging eyewitnesses to illegal activity, such as corruption or misuse of public resources, to contact and communicate with appropriate institutions in order to hold accountable those who abuse the public trust. The Order rests on the established principle that secrecy is the breeding ground for corruption and thus protects the right of every Iraqi to vigorously expose official wrongdoing at all levels of government in Iraq.

SECTION 2

PROHIBITIONS ON RETALIATION

1) No government employee or government contractor shall be discharged, demoted, transferred, threatened, intimidated, discriminated against, harassed, and/or otherwise retaliated against in any way ("Adverse Action") for reporting what he or she reasonably believes to be a violation of any law, rule, regulation, the Code for State Employees and Social Sector Discipline, Resolution No. 144, gross mismanagement, a gross waste of funds, an abuse of authority, a substantial and specific danger to health or safety, or any other "Corruption Case" as defined in Section 2.4 of Annex A to CPA Order No. 55 (CPA/ORD/27 January 2004/55), establishing the Commission on Public Integrity (collectively "Government Wrongdoing").

2) No Adverse Action shall be taken against any government employee or government contractor who cooperates with an investigation of or provides information to the Commission on Public Integrity, the Inspectors General of individual Ministries, the Board of Supreme Audit, or any other government entity charged with investigating and exposing evidence of illegal activity, public corruption, or official wrongdoing.

3) Sections 2.1 and 2.2 of this Order shall apply to Adverse Actions taken after the date this Order enters into force.

4) The provisions of Sections 2.1 and 2.2 shall not apply if the government can demonstrate that the decision to take the Adverse Action was not influenced in any way by the government employee's or government contractor's decision to report any Government Wrongdoing or to cooperate with or report information to any government entity charged with investigating and exposing evidence of illegal activity, public corruption, or official wrongdoing.

5) The provisions of Sections 2.1 and 2.2 shall not apply to persons who knowingly disclose false information or make false reports, make reports or disclose information that (from an objective viewpoint) is clearly untrue, or who make reports or disclose information about matters which by law cannot be reported or disclosed.

6) It shall be the government's burden to demonstrate that a person is not entitled to the protections of Sections 2.1 and 2.2 of this Order.

SECTION 3

REMEDIES AND PROCEDURES

1) Persons who violate Section 2 of this Order by taking an Adverse Action against government employees

or government contractors who report Government Wrongdoing or cooperate with, or report to, institutions charged with investigating and exposing corruption and official wrongdoing in Iraq shall:

> a) be liable to the aggrieved government employee or government contractor for money damages and any other relief deemed necessary by a court of competent jurisdiction to make an aggrieved government employee or government contractor whole, including reinstatement of employment with back pay; and/or b) be liable for criminal sanction in accordance with all applicable laws, regulations, and standards of procedural due process.

2) Government employees or government contractors alleging a violation of Section 2 of this Order must, within 90 days of the Adverse Action, file an Initial Complaint with the Inspector General appointed to their relevant ministry unless the Complaint relates to actions taken by a minister or the Inspector General. The Commission on Public Integrity shall promulgate procedures and regulations which permit Inspectors General to receive and investigate such Complaints. These procedures and regulations shall require Inspectors General to issue a Final Report that analyzes the merits of any Complaint within 60 days of filing and recommends whether: (i) to dismiss the Complaint, (ii) to pursue civil and/or criminal charges in a court of competent jurisdiction consistent with Section 3.1(b) of this Order, or (iii) to

take any other action deemed necessary under the particular facts and circumstances so long as such action is consistent with the law and due process.

3) Upon issuance of a Final Report, the Inspector General must forward it (and all accompanying records and files generated to create the Final Report) to the Commission on Public Integrity. The Commission on Public Integrity shall independently review the Final Report, records, and file and determine whether to adopt the Final Report in full, modify, wholly or partly reject, or resubmit the Final Report to the Inspector General with instructions. In the event the Complaint is dismissed, the aggrieved government employee or government contractor may bring a civil action in a court of competent jurisdiction seeking appropriate judicial relief. The court in such a case may consider the findings and analysis contained in the Final Report, as well as any additional findings and analysis rendered by the Commission on Public Integrity.

4) If the Inspector General fails to issue a Final Report within 60 days after the Complaint's filing, or the Commission on Public Integrity fails to make any determination about whether to adopt, modify, reject, or resubmit the Final Report within 30 days after its receipt, and there is no showing that such delays are due to the bad faith of the claimant, the claimant may (within 30 days after the passage of either deadline) bring a civil action in a court of competent jurisdiction seeking appropriate judicial relief. The institution of any such civil action under this paragraph shall

not prejudice the Inspector General from continuing its investigation and submitting its Final Report to the Commission on Public Integrity. The institution of any civil action under this paragraph shall not prejudice the Commission on Public Integrity from dismissing the Complaint, pursuing criminal penalties (as permitted under Sections 3 and 4 of this Order and Section 4 of Annex A to Order No. 55) against persons who violate Section 2 of this Order, or taking any other action deemed necessary under the particular facts.

5) The Commission on Public Integrity shall also promulgate procedures and regulations for receiving and investigating Complaints that relate to actions taken by ministers or Inspectors General. The regulations promulgated shall require the Commission on Public Integrity to analyze the merits of such Complaints and to issue a Final Report within 60 days of filing. Upon issuance of the Final Report, the Commission on Public Integrity shall: (i) dismiss the Complaint, (ii) pursue civil and/or criminal charges in a court of competent jurisdiction consistent with Section 3.1(b) of this Order, or (iii) take any other action (not including criminal or civil relief available in a court of competent jurisdiction) deemed necessary under the particular facts and circumstances so long as such action is consistent with law and due process. In the event the Complaint is dismissed, the aggrieved government employee or government contractor may bring a civil action in a court of competent jurisdiction seeking appropriate judicial relief. The court in such a case may consider the findings and analysis contained in the Final Report.

6) If the Commission on Public Integrity has not issued a Final Report within 60 days after the filing of a Complaint that relates to actions taken by a minister or an Inspector General and there is no showing that such delays are due to the bad faith of the aggrieved government employee or government contractor, then the aggrieved government employee or government contractor may bring a civil action in a court of competent jurisdiction seeking appropriate judicial relief.

1. Why does this bill claim that "secrecy is the breeding ground of corruption"?

2. What protections does this bill offer to whistleblowers?

"CLASSIFIED CONFUSION: WHAT LEAKS ARE BEING INVESTIGATED, AND WHAT'S THE LAW ON LEAKS?," BY CORA CURRIER, FOR *PROPUBLICA*, JULY 2, 2012

DESPITE THE FURIOUS BACK-AND-FORTH BETWEEN THE WHITE HOUSE AND REPUBLICAN LAWMAKERS OVER NATIONAL SECURITY LEAKS, THE PROSECUTION OF LEAKS ISN'T A SIMPLE MATTER.

Recent scoops on national security have drawn the ire of Republican lawmakers, who have accused the Obama White House of leaking stories that burnish its image.

Obama responded that he has "zero tolerance" for leaks. He also said: "the writers of these articles have all stated unequivocally that they didn't come from this White House. And that's not how we operate."

Someone somewhere has to be talking. Eric Holder said he's assigned two U.S. attorneys to lead separate criminal investigations into "potential unauthorized disclosures." Although the Justice Department won't comment on which particular leaks are under investigation, unnamed officials (of course) have given reporters an idea.

Here's what we know about leak investigations underway, the legality of leaks, and why leak prosecutions have been so rare.

LEAK: STUXNET

The *New York Times* reported that Obama ordered cyberattacks against Iran using Stuxnet, a computer virus the U.S. developed with Israel.

Sources: "participants" in the program and the attack, "members of the president's national security team," "current and former American, European and Israeli officials," "one of [Obama's] aides," "a senior administration official."

Investigation: The CIA reportedly sent a "crime report" to the Justice Department on the leak, and it is—as unnamed officials told Reuters—one of the two new investigations.

LEAK: FOILED UNDERWEAR BOMBER

The AP reported that the CIA foiled an Al-Qaeda plot out of Yemen to deploy a new kind of underwear bomb. Subsequent stories identified the role of a double-agent in stopping the plot.

Sources: "U.S. officials who were briefed on the operation."

Investigation: The story also apparently prompted the CIA to send a "crime report" to the Justice Department, making it the second of the criminal inquiries mentioned by Holder.

LEAK: THE CIA'S DRONE PROGRAM

The CIA's drone program and targeted strikes have been written about for years, but recent articles from *Newsweek* and the *New York Times* got particular attention.

Sources: Too many to count. The *Times* article alone cites "three dozen of [Obama's] current and former advisers." Staffers from the House and Senate Intelligence committees—whose members have been among the most vocal in their concern about leaks—were cited just last week in an article on CIA drone strikes.

Investigation: Apparently not. The CIA reportedly hasn't filed a report on drone leaks. Unnamed officials told Reuters one reason is that the CIA's drone program has already been so openly discussed (this despite the government's position in a separate case that the public doesn't know the program exists). A Justice Department official recently noted to Congress that agencies sometimes don't request an investigation because of "wide dissemination" of the leaked information.

WHAT LAWS HAVE LEAKERS VIOLATED?

There is no single law making the disclosure of any information stamped "classified" a crime. The Espionage Act has been used, though rarely, to prosecute the leaking of national security information. There are also laws on computer hacking and a patchwork of other statutes.

Under most of these laws, it's not enough to show that someone leaked—the government needs to prove they did so with intent or reason to believe that the information would hurt the U.S. or help a foreign country. Prosecutions of media leaks can also be hampered by First Amendment protections. In some cases the government has decided not to prosecute because classified information would be confirmed or further revealed in the process.

From 2005 to 2009, the Justice Department got 183 "crime reports" on leaks from others in the government. Those notifications led to 26 investigations. (The Justice Department can also start an independent investigation without a referral.) Obama has already brought six prosecutions under the Espionage Act, though many of the investigations were initiated under George W. Bush. Email and other technological changes have also made it easier, in some cases, to track leakers.

SO WHAT COMES NEXT?

If the Justice Department decides not to prosecute, the case goes back to the agency that reported it, which could take administrative steps to punish a leaker, anything from a reprimand to stripping security clearance. Many Republican senators have said the Justice Department isn't sufficiently independent to investigate potential White House leaks. Last week more than 30 senators sent a letter calling for a special counsel. They also suggested a congressional investigation could be launched.

In response to recent leaks, Director of National Intelligence James Clapper—who oversees the seventeen-agency intelligence community—issued a new directive asking the intelligence community's inspector general to lead further investigations in some cases where the Justice Department decides not to. Such an investigation wouldn't be a criminal inquiry, but it would reach beyond the scope of one agency. According to a DNI spokesman, the new investigative power wouldn't apply to leaks from the White House or non-intelligence agencies—but if the investigation pointed to a leaker outside the intelligence community, "there would be a process to make sure the employer was notified and could take their own steps."

The directive also mandates that intelligence employees getting periodic polygraph tests be asked if they've leaked information. Earlier this month, another DNI directive said personnel with access to national intelligence (and that's a lot of people) would be "continually evaluated and monitored."

Members of both the House and Senate have indicated they are working on legislation efforts to stem future leaks, but details are still unclear.

AREN'T LEAKS PAR FOR THE COURSE IN WASHINGTON?

That's part of the reason Congress hasn't made a comprehensive law penalizing them. In 2000, Bill Clinton vetoed a provision making it easier to prosecute leaks, saying it was too broad and would have had a "chilling effect" on legitimate communications.

Administrative penalties and the tools for criminal investigations that the government already has are sufficient, maintains Elizabeth Goitein, of the Brennan Center for Justice. Goitein says that new crackdowns could have an effect on would-be whistleblowers. Intelligence employees are specifically exempt from the Whistleblower Protection Act, which gives most government employees protection from retaliation for reporting wrongdoing. The government's position (as the DOJ told us in February) is that there are internal channels by which intelligence employees can report issues and the media is not one of them.

A spokesman for the DNI said that it was "the Director's number-one concern" that his new anti-leak policies were implemented without affecting whistleblowers.

1. Should Intelligence Agency employees be allowed to leak information to the media?

2. What kind of leaks would violate the Espionage Act?

"CHARTING OBAMA'S CRACKDOWN ON NATIONAL SECURITY LEAKS," BY CORA CURRIER, FROM *PROPUBLICA*, JULY 30, 2013

Chelsea Manning's conviction under the Espionage Act is the latest development in the Obama administration's push to prosecute leaks. We've updated our timeline with the most recent events.

Despite promises to strengthen protections for whistleblowers, the Obama administration has launched an aggressive crackdown on government employees who have leaked national security information to the press.

With charges filed against NSA leaker Edward Snowden this June, the administration has brought a total of seven cases under the Espionage Act, which dates from World War I and criminalizes disclosing information "relating to the national defense." Prior to the current administration, there had been only three known cases resulting in indictments in which the Espionage Act was used to prosecute government officials for leaks.

The administration has also targeted journalists. In May, it was revealed that the Department of Justice had secretly seized AP reporters' phone records while investigating a potential CIA leak, and targeted a Fox News reporter as part of a criminal leak case (outlined below). No journalist has been charged with a crime. But the news prompted an outcry that Obama's hard line on leaks could have a "chilling effect" on investigative reporting that depends on inside sources. (In response, the Justice Department issued new guidelines limiting when journalists' records can be sought.)

A spokesman for the Department of Justice told us the government "does not target whistleblowers." As they point out, government whistleblower protections shield only those who raise their concerns through the proper channels within their agency—not through leaks to the media or other unauthorized persons.

Director of National Intelligence James Clapper summed up the government's approach in a 2010 memo: "people in the intelligence business should be like my grandchildren—seen but not heard."

Here's a timeline of leak prosecutions under the Espionage Act, showing how they've picked up steam under Obama.

1971: DANIEL ELLSBERG AND ANTHONY RUSSO INDICTED

Daniel Ellsberg, Analyst for the military and RAND
Anthony Russo, RAND researcher

Two analysts at the RAND Corporation, Daniel Ellsberg and Anthony Russo, were indicted for leaking classified information about the Vietnam War—what came to be known as The Pentagon Papers. The case was dismissed in 1973 due to government misconduct.

1985: SAMUEL MORISON CONVICTED

Samuel Morison, Civilian analyst

Samuel Loring Morison, a civilian analyst with the Navy, was convicted of leaking classified satellite photographs to a British magazine. He was sentenced to 2 years in prison, and eventually pardoned by President Bill Clinton in 2001.

AUGUST 2005: LAWRENCE FRANKLIN INDICTED

Lawrence Franklin, State Department analyst

Franklin, an analyst for the State Department, was charged with leaking classified information about Iran to two lobbyists for AIPAC.

JANUARY 2006: LAWRENCE FRANKLIN CONVICTED

Franklin pled guilty and was sentenced to 12 years in prison, which was later reduced to ten months' house arrest. The two lobbyists were also indicted for receiving unauthorized information—a highly unusual charge—but the case against them was dropped in May of 2009.

APRIL 2010: THOMAS DRAKE INDICTED

National Security Agency employee Thomas Drake was charged with violating the Espionage Act for retaining classified documents for "unauthorized disclosure." He was suspected to have leaked information on the agency's surveillance program TrailBlazer. The case against Drake began under the Bush administration - FBI agents raided his house in 2007.

MAY 2010: SHAMAI LEIBOWITZ CONVICTED

Shamai Leibowitz, FBI translator

Leibowitz, a linguist and translator for the FBI, pleaded guilty to leaking classified information to a blogger. He was sentenced to 20 months in prison. At the time of his sentencing, not even the judge knew exactly what he had leaked, though later disclosures indicated it was FBI wiretaps of conversations between Israeli diplomats about Iran.

JUNE 2010: CHELSEA MANNING ARRESTED

Chelsea Manning, Army intelligence analyst

Chelsea Manning, a 22-year Army Private, was arrested after she told someone online that she was the source for Wikileaks' biggest gets, including a quarter-million State Department cables.

It will be more almost two years before she is ultimately charged in a military court. In February 2013, she pleaded guilty to providing files to Wikileaks, but not to violating the Espionage Act and other charges. Courts have maintained an unprecedented level of secrecy over the case, withholding documents and allowing witnesses to testify in secret.

AUGUST 2010: STEPHEN KIM INDICTED

Stephen Kim, State Department analyst

Kim, an analyst working under contract with the State Department, was indicted for giving classified information to Fox News about North Korea. His case is still pending. In a July 2013 ruling in the case, a federal judge said the government did not need to show that the information leaked could have damaged national security – just that Kim knew it could and willfully leaked the information.

The Washington Post reported in May 2013 that Fox News journalist James Rosen was investigated in the Kim case. The Department seized Rosen's phone records and emails, and tracked his "comings and goings from the State Department." Rosen was not charged with a crime, but an FBI investigator wrote that there was evidence he was a "co-conspirator."

DECEMBER 2010: JEFFREY STERLING INDICTED

Jeffrey Sterling, CIA officer

Sterling, a CIA officer, was charged with leaking information about the CIA's efforts against Iran's nuclear program. His case is still pending.

New York Times reporter James Risen was ordered to testify in Sterling's trial. Prosecutors believed Kim had leaked material to Risen for his book, "State of War." Risen fought the subpoena, arguing that it was his First Amendment right to protect his source's confidentiality. In July 2013, Risen lost that fight, when a federal appeals court said there was no "reporters privilege" that could allow him not to testify.

JUN. 2011: CASE AGAINST THOMAS DRAKE DROPPED

Drake pled guilty to a minor charge, not under the Espionage Act, and served no prison time. The government had decided that they could not prosecute him without revealing details about the documents he supposedly leaked. Critics saw the government's withdrawal as a sign that they had over-reached in using the Espionage Act.

JANUARY 2012: JOHN KIRIAKOU CHARGED

John Kiriakou, former CIA officer

John Kiriakou was charged with leaking information about the interrogation of an Al Qaeda leader and disclosing the name of a CIA analyst involved. Kiriakou gave an interview on ABC News in 2007 detailing the Bush administration's use of waterboarding in interrogating terrorist suspects.

OCTOBER 2012: JOHN KIRIAKOU CONVICTED

Kiriakou pleaded guilty to disclosing the name of a covert CIA officer. He was convicted of violating the

Intelligence Identities Protection Act, the first under the law in 27 years. In January, Kiriakou was sentenced to 2 1/2 years in prison.

JUNE 14, 2013: EDWARD SNOWDEN CHARGED

Edward Snowden, Former NSA Contractor

Edward Snowden, who leaked documents about the NSA's secret surveillance programs, was charged with theft of government property and two counts of disclosing information under the Espionage Act – charges which together carry a penalty of up to 30 years in prison.

JULY 30, 2013: CHELSEA MANNING CONVICTED

A military tribunal judge found Manning not guilty of aiding the enemy – the most serious charge against her. She was found guilty of multiple counts under the Espionage Act and five counts of theft, among other charges. She could spend decades in prison.

Christie Thompson contributed to this story.

STATEMENT FROM THE DEPARTMENT OF JUSTICE:

The Justice Department has always taken seriously cases in which government employees and contractors entrusted with classified information are suspected of willfully disclosing such classified information to those not entitled to it. As a general matter, prosecutions of whose who leaked classified information to reporters have been rare, due, in part, to the inherent challenges involved in identifying the person responsible for the illegal disclosure and in compiling the evidence necessary to prove it beyond a reasonable doubt in a court of law. Prosecutorial decisions are always based on the facts, the evidence and the law. The Department has been working with the intelligence community not only to expedite but also to improve the handling of such cases. The Justice Department has also been working with these agencies to ensure that that the intelligence community and other agencies have remedies of their own to address employees suspected of leaking classified information in those instances where criminal prosecution is not feasible.

The Justice Department does not target whistleblowers. Should any federal employee wish to blow the whistle or report government wrongdoing, there are well-established mechanisms for doing so with the Offices of Inspector General of their respective agencies. With regard to classified information, there is a particular statute providing lawful mechanisms for reporting such matters. We always encourage federal employees to do so. However, we cannot sanction or condone federal employees who knowingly and willfully disclose classified information to the media or others not entitled to receive such information. An individual in authorized possession of classified information has no authority or right to unilaterally determine that classified information should be made public or disclosed to those not entitled to it. The leaker is not the owner of such information and only the owner can declassify such information.

As a general matter and as provided by the law, federal regulations and Justice Department guidelines, whenever the Justice Department conducts an investigation of this sort, we seek to strike the proper balance between First Amendment freedoms and the law enforcement and national security interest in investigating unauthorized disclosures of classified information. In recognition of the importance of freedom of the press to a free and democratic society, it is the Justice Department's policy that the prosecutorial power of the government should not be used in such a way that it impairs a reporter's responsibility to cover as broadly as possible controversial public issues.

1. What is the US Justice Department's position on federal whistleblowers?

2. Should journalists be protected when they report on leaked classified information?

CHAPTER 4

WHAT ADVOCACY GROUPS SAY

Whistleblowers play an important role in exposing corruption and illegal activity. However, some data leaks can have unintended negative effects, such as publishing civilians' personally identifiable information. While corruption does need to be exposed, people's personal data must still be protected. Activist organizations like The National Whistleblower Center and the Sunlight Foundation are committed to supporting and protecting whistleblowers while also guiding them on ways to leak ethically.

Activist organizations can also be formed or motivated by information learned from whistleblowers. After Edward Snowden blew the whistle on the NSA's mass surveillance, civil rights organizations like the American Civil Liberties Union (ACLU) and the Sunlight Foundation called for stronger privacy rights. As you will read in this chapter, Snowden's NSA revelation caused activists all over the globe to unite and demand an end to mass surveillance programs worldwide. Activist organizations seek to hold the government accountable for instances of corruption uncovered from whistleblowers.

"WHISTLEBLOWER POLICY," BY THE WIKIMEDIA FOUNDATION

We're serious about legal compliance and we're serious about protecting whistleblowers who in good faith bring instances of possible unlawful conduct or financial wrong-doing to our attention. Our trustees, officers, employees, volunteers, and independent contractors hired to perform services at the Wikimedia Foundation (WMF) must comply with applicable laws and regulations in the conduct of their duties and responsibilities. This whistleblower policy applies to all such individuals.

We all share responsibility for ensuring that our workplace is free from unlawful conduct and financial wrongdoing. If you receive a complaint covered by this policy, or if you witness any conduct you reasonably believe may be covered by this policy, we expect you in good faith to report that complaint or conduct, and we encourage you to use the channels set forth in this policy. We also expect our employees and all others connected with WMF to fully cooperate with any investigations of complaints.

SCOPE AND OBJECTIVES

This policy sets out the reporting procedures and whistleblower protections connected with complaints about potential legal violations and financial wrongdoing. It does not cover all types of complaints or misconduct, though the other policies that govern such complaints and misconduct also rigorously protect from retaliation those who make good faith reports/complaints. For example, sexual harassment, discrimination, disputes with a co-worker, and various types of conflicts of interest are covered by other policies. Those complaints may trigger different channels of reporting or investigation and should be reported to specific members of the Talent & Culture department or to the appropriate individual or department, as set out under the relevant policy.

The main objectives of this whistleblower policy are to:

1. Encourage good faith reporting of suspected (a) illegal activity, or (b) fraudulent, dishonest, or unethical misuse of resources or property of WMF; and

2. Protect those who report in good faith such activities to us or who use other reporting channels available under applicable law or regulations.

While this policy provides a reporting mechanism to alert WMF of any concerns, you may have additional reporting channels and rights under applicable local, state, or federal laws and regulations, including reporting directly to law enforcement. Nonetheless, we encourage you to file reports under this policy to ensure WMF can fully investigate your concerns.

REPORTING PROCESS

WHAT SHOULD YOU REPORT?

As noted, if you reasonably and in good faith believe that you have witnessed or been informed about potentially unlawful conduct or misuse of WMF resources or property, you should report such instances. We encourage you to use the WMF channels stated under this policy to report any policy, practice, or conduct of WMF that you reasonably believe to be (a) illegal activity under applicable local, state, or federal laws and regulations; or (b) fraudulent, dishonest, or unethical misuse of resources or property of WMF, including but not limited to, misappropriation of funds; falsification of financial records; fraudulent financial reporting or actions that may lead to such fraudulent reporting; destroying, altering, concealing, or falsifying a document or official proceeding; fraudulently influencing or misleading any independent public accountant engaged in the performance of an audit of WMF's financial statements; or any other form of financial impropriety (this is not meant to be an exhaustive list but rather a guide to the types of improper behavior covered by this policy).

WHO MAY SUBMIT A REPORT?

WMF Trustees, officers, employees, volunteers, and independent contractors hired to perform services at the Wikimedia Foundation (WMF).

HOW DO YOU SUBMIT A REPORT?

With respect to reports made within WMF under this policy, you may report your concerns verbally or in writing to any one of the following: your manager, the supervisor of your manager, a designated individual in the Talent & Culture department (namely, the Chief Talent and Culture Officer, the Chargée d'Affaires, or the People Relations and Inclusion Lead), the Chief Financial Officer, the General Counsel, the Executive Director, the Chair of the Audit Committee, or the Chair of the Board of Trustees. You may also report your concerns anonymously through our hotline with an independent service.

If the subject of your report is the Executive Director, you may report your concerns directly to the Chair of the Audit Committee or the Chair of the Board of Trustees. If the subject of any report is the Chair of the Audit Committee, you may report your concerns directly to the Chair of the Board of Trustees.

WHAT HAPPENS AFTER A REPORT IS SUBMITTED?

All reports will be subject to an initial assessment. Assuming the report falls within this policy, it shall be handled by the Chair of the Audit Committee, who is responsible for overseeing assessments and investigations of concerns about potentially unlawful activity or misuse of WMF resources or property reported under this policy. As noted above, if the subject of any report is the Chair of the Audit Committee, the report may be forwarded directly to the Chair of the Board of Trustees.

The Chair of the Audit Committee may request the assistance of others, including the General Counsel, the Chief Financial Officer, other members of the Audit Committee, other staff members, and potentially outside counsel in the investigation and resolution of the report. However, no trustee, officer, or staff member may participate in the investigation of a report of which he or she is the subject, or be present at any deliberation or vote.

All concerns of unlawful conduct forwarded to the Chair of the Audit Committee will be promptly assessed and investigated and, when warranted, corrective action may be taken.

CONFIDENTIALITY

Reports covered by this policy will be kept confidential to the extent possible, consistent with conducting a complete and fair investigation and achieving an appropriate resolution. This may require sharing the information in the report with other people, such as appropriate staff members, other witnesses, the Board of Trustees, the Audit Committee, and WMF's outside accountants and lawyers.

Unless you submit your concerns anonymously, we will notify you about what actions will be taken (or not taken) to the extent that is reasonably possible and consistent with any privacy or confidentiality limitations. If there will be no further action or investigation, we will also provide an explanation to you to the extent that is reasonably possible and consistent with any privacy or confidentiality limitations.

WHAT IS THE DIFFERENCE BETWEEN REPORTING "ANONYMOUSLY" AND REPORTING "CONFIDENTIALLY"?

If you submit your report anonymously, we will not know your identity to the extent your report does not contain details that might identify you. All reports (and your identity, if you choose to disclose it) will be kept confidential within the reporting channel, consistent with our obligation to conduct a complete and fair investigation. We will share your report or otherwise disclose your report as appropriate only to conduct a complete and fair investigation and achieve an appropriate resolution, to review WMF operations in general, or to comply with applicable law.

PROTECTION FROM RETALIATION

Consistent with this policy and applicable law, WMF will not discharge, demote, suspend, threaten, harass, or retaliate against you based on the fact that you (a) acted in accordance with this policy, when done in good faith; or (b) exercised your rights under local, state, or federal laws and regulations.

Activities protected from retaliation include:

1. Submitting reasonable, good faith reports under this policy;

2. Initiating, testifying in, assisting or otherwise participating in any investigation, lawsuit, or administrative action regarding violations of local, state, or federal laws and regulations;

3. Providing, or expressing an intention to provide, in good faith a law enforcement officer with information relating to the commission or possible commission of any violation of local, state, or federal laws and regulations;

4. Refusing to participate in any activity that is a fraudulent, dishonest, or unethical misuse of resources or property of WMF and filing a report about this issue in accordance with this policy; and/or

5. Refusing to participate in any illegal activity in violation of applicable local, state, or federal laws and regulations.

If you reasonably believe you have been retaliated against in violation of this policy, you should follow the procedures for filing a report to any of the departments or individuals set out above. Any individual within WMF is subject to discipline if they retaliate against another individual who has reported in good faith a potential violation covered by this policy, who has cooperated in the investigation of such a violation, or who has otherwise acted in good faith in accordance with the terms of this policy.

1. Should whistleblowers be allowed to remain anonymous?

2. According to the Wikimedia Foundation (WMF) what kind of information should be reported?

"SENATE LAUNCHES BIPARTISAN WHISTLEBLOWER PROTECTION CAUCUS," BY MATT RUMSEY, FROM THE SUNLIGHT FOUNDATION, FEBRUARY 26, 2015

A bipartisan group of Senators came together yesterday to launch the Senate Whistleblower Protection Caucus. Led by Sens. Chuck Grassley, R-Iowa, and Ron Wyden, D-Ore., the caucus' aim is to serve as a resource for Senate offices that are interested in whistleblower issues.

According to Grassley, the caucus chair, the group will "help create a culture where the contributions of whistleblowers are valued and their rights respected." To this end, the caucus plans to offer training and consult Senate offices on how to handle whistleblower disclosures and protect whistleblowers from retaliation. It will also serve as a clearinghouse for information on whistleblower issues.

The Government Accountability Project came out with a strong endorsement of the caucus, noting that "historically, whistleblower protections have enjoyed bipartisan support". The caucus' founding members include Republican Sens. Ron Johnson, Wis., Mark Kirk, Ill., Deb Fischer, Neb., and Thom Tillis, N.C., as well as Democrats Barbara Boxer, Calif., Claire McCaskill, Mo., Tammy Baldwin, Wis., and Ed Markey, Mass.

We are happy to see senators standing up for the rights of whistleblowers, who often put their careers on the line to expose instances of fraud and abuse within the government and ensure that valuable information is not unnecessarily withheld from the public.

1. Why is it important to create a culture that values whistleblowers?

2. Why is it important for whistleblower protections to have bipartisan support?

"GETTING SECRECY OUT OF SCIENCE" BY SEAN VITKA, FROM THE SUNLIGHT FOUNDATION, MAY 22, 2014

The National Institute of Standards and Technology (NIST) is responsible for developing scientific measurements and standards for the government. Because of that immense responsibility, its recommendations are adopted across the world. This includes cutting-edge development of cryptography, otherwise known as the magic that keeps the Internet and your computer safe.

This is why it was so brutally disappointing when the Snowden leaks revealed that the NSA had subverted NIST's rule-promulgation process, secretly weakening the math that individuals, companies and governments around the world rely on for informational security. That secrecy is unacceptable, and that squandering of NIST's international integrity is a stunning disappointment.

It is the kind of secrecy that is anathema to Sunlight's mission and values.

Last month, Sunlight signed onto a coalition letter arguing that NIST should avoid consultation with the National Security Agency (NSA) when developing standards and, when it must, the process should be public and transparent. Since then, Sunlight has been working with our allies to accomplish that.

Last night, the House Committee on Science, Space, and Technology adopted an amendment authored by Rep. Alan Grayson, D-Fla., and supported by Sunlight and some of our colleagues that limits the NSA's influence on NIST.

Grayson's amendment removes the requirement that NIST consult with NSA, which has been mandatory under the Frontiers in Innovation, Research, Science and Technology Act since 1987. NIST can now choose to consult with the NSA when they decide the advice will be useful, but will not be forced to do so — or feel pressure to adhere to the NSA's demands.

This is one of the first successful legislative steps toward limiting the NSA since it came into existence. There's far more to be done here: to ensure that when NIST does consult with the NSA, the process maintains the integrity and openness Americans deserve; and to vastly improve the oversight that has apparently failed to limit the NSA's ambitions.

Still, this amendment is a strong rebuttal to the NSA's abuse of its position within the political system.

1. Should the National Institute of Standards and Technology (NIST) be forced to consult with the NSA?

2. Is lack of transparency surrounding the NSA's dealings with the NIST potentially harmful to Americans?

"ON 1ST ANNIVERSARY OF SNOWDEN REVELATIONS, WORLD GOVERNMENTS URGED TO END MASS SURVEILLANCE," BY *ADVOX*, JUNE 5, 2014

A huge international gathering of experts have called on world governments to adopt the 13 International Principles on the Application of Human Rights to Communications Surveillance (IPAHRCS) — principles aimed at putting an end to the blanket surveillance of law-abiding persons. The call comes a year to the day after whistleblower Edward Snowden first revealed details about how government spy agencies, including the United States' National Security Agency (NSA), are monitoring law-abiding citizens on a massive and unprecedented scale. In the 12 months since the revelations, most world governments have ignored growing calls from citizens to put an end to these activities.

The group of over 450 organizations and experts, supported by over 350,000 individuals from across the globe, have been calling for the adoption of new rules to protect innocent citizens from government spying. The 13 International Principles establish clear guidelines to ensure government surveillance activities are consistent with human rights. These principles were developed over months of consultation with technology, privacy, and human rights experts from around the world. The principles emphasize the human rights obligations of governments engaged in communications surveillance.

Group members are also recommending greater use of software libre, decentralized architectures, and end-to-end encryption to help safeguard citizens' privacy rights. They say citizens deserve strong data protection safeguards to safeguard their privacy from government monitoring.

Here's what International experts are saying about the Necessary and Proportionate Principles, and the need to end mass surveillance:

LATIN AMERICA

Luis Fernando García, R3D (Mexico):
"The 13 Principles are defenders of an Internet that constitutes a space for the exercise of human rights. By promoting its recognition, we reject the false choice between security and privacy and, at the same time, we defend the democratic aspirations of our societies."

Paulo Renán da Silva Santarém (Brasil):
"Edward Snowden's revelations were crucial in ensuring that civil society had enough evidence to pressure our government for the approval of Marco Civil. Certainly,

now is time for the Brazilian Government to take the lead by implementing the 13 Principles into domestic law, specifically against mass data retention."

Pilar Saenz, RedPaTodos (Colombia):
"We insist that surveillance must be 'necessary and proportionate' and with independent oversight to prevent abuse of power."

Joana Varon, Center for Technology and Society (Brazil):
"Snowden has provided us with the most powerful tool of our current era: information. Every single Internet user around the world should feel empowered by that and, as such, push for a change in current surveillance practices. Mass surveillance has nothing to do with security, it represents a serious threat to fundamental human rights. Any surveillance practice should be limited to what is necessary and proportionate, and that's why the 13 principles should be the starting point."

Ramiro Álvarez Ugarte, Asociación por los Derechos Civiles (Argentina):
"A year ago, we confirmed what many suspected. Now we know that basic human rights are being violated due to a wide system of mass surveillance which simply is incompatible with a free and democratic society. While Snowden has shed light onto these practices, in Latin America we remain in the dark. Unchecked and autonomous intelligence agencies engage in political surveillance all the time, as recent scandals in Colombia and Argentina have clearly shown. Massive or not, this kind of surveillance puts a check on demo-

cratic participation and region-wide reform efforts are as urgent as necessary."

Valeria Betancourt, Association for Progressive Communications (Ecuador – International):
"It is necessary to reinforce the call to states to take measures that will put an end to privacy violations and ensure that legislation and practices related to communications surveillance, collection of personal data, and interception of communications, adhere to international human rights. A robust protection for human rights is a condition for democracy."

Jacobo Nájera, free software developer [Latin America]:
"Snowden highlights the capabilities of the most powerful system of mass surveillance; and has reaffirmed that mass surveillance and the centralization of development processes and services on the Internet destroy the Net as we know it. There is a need to use and develop free software, end-to-end encryption, and decentralized services."

Ivan Martínez, President, Wikimedia Mexico (Mexico):
"Freedom on the internet is an essential component of the Wikimedia projects, and a value that governs their overall performance. Its defense in the social context is a necessary task in many societies because of the temptations of certain political figures to place barriers on its development. As Wikipedians and promoters of free knowledge, in previous years we didn't consider it right to passively observe possible attempts to monitor peoples' actions on the net, and we always support efforts to guarantee a free internet without any kind of surveillance."

Claudio Ruiz, ONG Derechos Digitales (Latin America):
"Snowden's revelations illustrate the significance of human rights on the Internet. In the post-Snowden era, states are not the only enemies to our civil liberties, private companies are as well. The fragility of our rights in the light of technological developments is to require all actors unrestricted commitment to protecting the privacy of all."

Katitza Rodriguez, International Rights Director, EFF (Peru-International):
"As our everyday interactions, activities, and communications now emit a continuous stream of revealing information, the question has become: how do we preserve fundamental freedoms in the digital age?" EFF International Rights Director Katitza Rodriguez said. "The 13 Principles explain how and why we must rein in unchecked surveillance state at home and abroad and protect the freedoms of everyone, regardless of citizenship or statelessness."

NORTH AMERICA

Steve Anderson, OpenMedia Executive Director (Canada – International):
"These 13 Principles represent the positive alternative to secretive and unaccountable mass surveillance. We all need to work together to rein in out-of-control government surveillance by making sure it is necessary, proportionate, and respects our fundamental human rights. Everyone deserves to keep their private life private and it's past time decision-makers listened to citizens and implemented these common sense international principles."

Jochai Ben-Avie, Policy Director, Access (United States – International):

"The human rights that are negatively impacted by surveillance are some of the most treasured and the most easily invaded. The 13 Principles provide a framing against which government surveillance practices around the world can be measured and they are already affecting change around the world. The Principles are a rallying cry for human rights defenders, and the chorus of users who have already spoken out demonstrate that no longer will the public acquiesce quietly to mass surveillance. As we mark the one year anniversary of the first Snowden revelation and reflect on what we know now, we can see that the Principles have fundamentally changed the discourse and are one of the most powerful tools in the fight to limit how States spy on the users of the world."

Cindy Cohn, Legal Director, EFF (United States):

"Human rights law already strongly protects the privacy and free expression of people around the world, but the dramatically increased ability and willingness of the NSA, along with its counterparts, to engage in mass surveillance and to undermine online security required specific thinking about how to apply and preserve this important law in this radically new context. The 13 Principles accomplish this goal, providing a guidestar for nongovernmental organizations and governments around the world who want to ensure the ongoing protection of our fundamental freedoms in the digital age. They also serve as an important complement to the work that EFF and others are doing domestically in the US to try to rein in the NSA."

Tamir Israel, Staff Lawyer, Samuelson-Glushko Canadian Internet Policy & Public Interest Clinic (CIPPIC)(Canada): The long string of Snowden revelations have confirmed for us that the worst case scenario is true: state agencies have transformed our digital networks into a means of mass surveillance. If permitted to stand, this state of affairs threatens the very foundations of democracy by subverting our most powerful vehicle for those wishing to challenge prevailing opinion. It is incumbent on us to fix this problem, and the solution requires dynamic political, technical and legal solutions. The Necessary & Proportionate Principles address the last of these by reasserting privacy and other human rights in a way that is meaningful in this new technological era. They are designed to bring us back to a world where surveillance occurs only when it is needed and justifiable and to put an end to the current 'collect everything' reality that has crept up on us in recent years.

Christopher Parsons, Postdoctoral Fellow, Citizen Lab, Munk School of Global Affairs, University of Toronto (Canada): "The past year has revealed that dragnet state surveillance has enveloped the world despite our nations' privacy and data protection laws, laws that have demonstrably been diminished, undermined, and evaded by privacy-hostile governments over the course of the past decade. It is critical that we take the initiative and work to better endow our privacy commissioners and data protection regulators with the powers they need to investigate and terminate programs that inappropriately or unlawfully invade and undermine our individual and collective rights to privacy".

Yana Welinder, Legal Counsel, Wikimedia Foundation (United States):
"Untargeted surveillance means that people cannot anonymously share their wisdom online or freely read without the fear of constantly being watched. It's a threat to the very core of what makes us human — the drive to think and formulate ideas. The 13 Principles push back on that threat. They demand that governments avoid excessive surveillance and respect human rights."

Yochai Benkler, Professor, Harvard Law School and Berkman Center for Internet and Society (United States):
"Because mass surveillance is technically difficult, legally suspect, and social taboo in democratic societies, the national security establishment has had to break or warp all other major systems in society to achieve it. What we learned from Snowden is that the ambition of the national security establishment has subverted open technical systems and the professional norms-based processes that undergird our technical infrastructure; undermined markets and commercial innovation; and produced a theatre of the grotesque where public accountability and judicial, executive, and legislative control should have been."

Eben Moglen, President and Executive Director of the Software Freedom Law Center (International):
"If—by technical, legal and political means—we prevent centralized control and surveillance of the Net, we save liberty. If not, unshakeable despotism lies in the human future".

Cynthia Wong, Human Rights Watch (United States – International):

"The Internet has become central to our lives. But the NSA and GCHQ's 'collect it all' attitude makes it incredibly hard for human rights defenders, journalists, and ordinary citizens worldwide to go online without fear. To accept these agencies' arguments for mass surveillance without challenge means the beginning of the end of privacy in the digital age."

AFRICA

Arthur Gwagwa, Zimbabwe Human Rights Forum (Zimbawe):

"As the evolution of digital technologies outpaces international and regional regulatory consensus, the 13 Principles collect what little there is in the form of guidance, and proactively go beyond that by providing a sturdy, timeless, and universal framework within which national, regional, and international reforms on the pre- senting issues can sit and find strength."

Hisham Almiraat, Global Voices Advocacy (Morocco, International):

"The advent of the internet marked a major milestone for human rights activists in some of the most repressive places on earth. It symbolized an unprecedented extension of the public sphere and a serious blow to governments' attempts to curtail freedom of speech. Mass, indiscriminate surveillance is threatening to destroy this progress. The 13 Principles offer a workable solution to balance security and privacy. We call upon all governments to adopt these principles in order to protect their citizens' right to privacy and freedom of speech."

EUROPE

Simon Davies, Publisher, "The Privacy Surgeon" (United Kingdom – International):
"The majority of the world's governments have responded with either orchestrated deception or brazen indifference to the Snowden revelations. A year on, the secret arrangements that enabled the creation of a vast global spying regime continue almost unchanged. Initiatives such as the 13 Principles – and the huge coalition that supports them – can make a real difference to an arrogant and unaccountable spy empire that imperils the privacy of everyone."

Stuart Hamilton, Director of Policy and Advocacy, International Federation of Library Associations and Institutions (International):
"For librarians, safeguarding the privacy of our users is a crucial professional principle. When people are under surveillance, they lose their ability to think freely—nobody likes to read with someone looking over their shoulder. The 13 Principles show us the way to ensure existing human rights law applies to modern digital surveillance. IFLA is proud to be a signatory."

Christian Horchert, CCC (Germany):
"Snowden helped us to understand on what fragile foundation our information society is build upon. We are at a turning point where we need to decide how to move

forward: Do we really want to live in a world of insecurity and mistrust or not?"

Joe McNamee, European Digital Rights, Executive Director (European Union):
"We have slipped unconsciously into a world where basic concepts of democracy and the rule of law have been replaced by sophistry and impunity. The 13 Principles draw a clear baseline on which democratic principles, privacy and freedom of communication can be rebuilt.

Carly Nyst, Legal Director, Privacy International (United Kingdom – International):
"The 13 Principles have completely changed the debate around communications surveillance. By providing a detailed, clear interpretation of human rights standards that is relevant and meaningful in the digital age, the 13 Principles have done what so many national legislatures have failed to do—update long-standing legal protections of the right to privacy in the light of new technologies that challenge traditional distinctions such as content vs metadata, nationals vs non-nationals, intelligence vs. law enforcement. The 13 Principles are the most important tool that civil society has to mould the crucial debate being had, in the aftermath of the Snowden revelations, about the limits of state power to spy on citizens around the world."

Danny O'Brien, International Director, Electronic Frontier Foundation, (United Kingdom – International):
"The application of international law has lagged for years behind the technological advances which have led to

our current global surveillance state. The 13 Principles spells out exactly how we can update our understanding of human rights to combat this erosion of civil liberties. As courts around the world begin to tackle these issues seriously, it's invaluable for them to have such timely and precise guidance."

John Ralston Saul, President, PEN International (International):

"The principles of expression are simple—maximum transparency in places of power, maximum free expression for citizens. Privacy is a key part of free expression. In private we work out what we will say and do in public. The growing use of secrecy and surveillance by governments and corporations is a direct attack on free expression. The use of fear to justify this secrecy and surveillance is a cynical diversion from the central issue. Free expression."

Katarzyna Szymielewicz, President, Panoptykon Foundation (Poland):

"In the aftermath of Snowden's disclosures, civil society organizations have to speak with one voice to remind governments across the world what principles should apply when it comes to surveillance. The 13 Principles make it very clear that there is no way of reconciling mass, preemptive surveillance with the right to privacy and human rights safeguards such as presumption of innocence. The manifesto with 13 principles is our way of communicating these core values to decision makers and the media. However, we expect much more than public debate: we demand their implementation."

Friedhelm Weinberg, HURIDOCS (Germany):
"There has been an incredible gap between the practices of mass surveillance and the protections everyone
ought to enjoy under international human rights law. The
13 Principles have been the one crucial document that
has fueled the process of addressing this gap, and clos-
ing it. Unlawful mass surveillance still occurs, but the
13 Principles are now so widely recognized that there will
be no more excuses for everyone—government, businesses or others—not to do more to protect the rights of
individuals around the globe."

Jérémie Zimmermann, La Quadrature du Net (France):
"Our humanities are now indivisible from the Machine, we
became the Cyborg. And now we see that the machine as
a whole has been subverted to work against us, to spy
on us and control us. We must fight back for our humanities against this oppressive Machine, with software libre,
decentralized architectures, and end-to-end encryption."

ASIA

Professor Kyung Sin Park, Open Net (South Korea):
"The 13 Principles are the first attempt to create an international legal standard on the right to be free from surveillance, that is, surveillance by any government on any private person on earth via any communications medium."

Sana Saleem, Bolo Bhi (Pakistan):
"The Snowden revelations were instrumental in exposing the
corporate-government nexus that enables surveillance. The
Necessary & Proportionate Principles are a much-needed

step towards limiting states' power to infringe on our right to privacy."

OCEANIA

Joy Liddicoat, Association for Progressive Communications (New Zealand – International):
"The revelations of whistleblowers, including Edward Snowden, have shone a bright light into the dark interior workings of modern democracies, revealing the deeply uncomfortable truth that our human rights are at grave risk at home from those elected to represent democratic values, including human rights to privacy. We do not want our governments to protect us—we want them to protect our rights, but when they will not, civil society voices and leadership must respond emphatically. The 13 Principles provide a clear set of guidance for the application and upholding of human rights in a digital age in relation to surveillance."

1. Why are activists calling for an end to mass surveillance?

2. What effects does mass surveillance have on the right to privacy?

"LOOKING BACK ONE YEAR AFTER THE EDWARD SNOWDEN DISCLOSURES - AN INTERNATIONAL PERSPECTIVE," BY KATITZA RODRIGUEZ, FROM THE ELECTRONIC FRONTIER FOUNDATION, MAY 15, 2014

June 5th marks the first anniversary of the beginning of the Edward Snowden revelations–a landmark event in global awareness of the worldwide spying machine. It has been a year where the world has learned specific details of how the NSA and its four closest allies in the Five Eyes partnership (United Kingdom, Canada, Australia, and New Zealand) have been spying on much of the world's digital communications. What have we learned?

"The US government had built a system that has as its goal the complete elimination of electronic privacy worldwide" — Glenn Greenwald, *No Place to Hide: Edward Snowden, the NSA, and the U.S. Surveillance State*

The foreign intelligence agencies of these nations have constructed a web of interoperability at the technical and operational levels that spans the entire globe. We have learned the extent of the cooperation and intelligence sharing amongst these countries, and have witnessed how material gathered under one country's surveillance regime is readily shared with the others. The strategic location of the Five Eyes countries enables

132

them to surveil much of the world's Internet traffic as it transits through their hubs and is stored in their various territories. Moreover, they have partnered with over 80 major global corporations to leverage their spying capabilities. The scope and reach of their cooperation and intelligence sharing has shocked the world, including many who were previously unaware of the privacy threats that EFF has been covering since 2005.

In a document disclosed this year, the NSA defined their "collection posture" as, "Sniff, know, collect, process, exploit, partner it all." This last year, we have learned that the NSA has strayed far from its legitimate goal of protecting national security. In fact, we have seen the NSA participate in economic espionage, diplomatic spying and suspicionless surveillance of entire populations. Even worse, the NSA has also surreptitiously weakened the products and standards that Internet users use to protect themselves against online spying.

In his new book about working with Snowden, *No Place To Hide*, journalist Glenn Greenwald lays out some alarming facts that have been revealed in the year of leaks:

- In a 30 day period beginning on March 2013, the NSA collected almost 3 billion telephone calls and emails that had passed directly through US telecom networks. As Greenwald explained, that "exceeds the collection of each of the systems from Russia, Mexico, and virtually all countries in Europe, and roughly equal to the collection of data from China."
- In a 30 day period, a single NSA unit had collected data on more than 97 billion emails and 124 billion phone calls from around the world.

- In a single 30 day period, the NSA has collected 500 million pieces of data from Germany, 2.3 billion from Brazil, and 13.5 billion from India.
- The NSA has collected 70 million pieces of metadata in cooperation with France, 60 million with Spain, 47 million with Italy, 1.8 million with the Netherlands, 33 million with Norway, and 23 million with Denmark.

In addition, the Snowden report has brought to light additional details of the long-known three-tiered hierarchy of NSA partnerships with foreign governments. As reported by Greenwald's book:

TIER 1: Five Eyes is an agreement between the US and United Kingdom, Canada, Australia, and New Zealand to collaborate on global spying while voluntarily restricting their own spying on one another unless specifically requested to do so by a partner country's own officials.

TIER 2: Countries that the NSA works with for specific surveillance projects while also spying heavily on them. For example, these include mostly European countries (Austria, Belgium, Czech Republic, Denmark, Germany, Greece, Hungary, Iceland, Italy, Luxembourg, Netherlands, Norway, Poland, Portugal, Spain, Sweden, Switzerland, Turkey). Some Asian countries (Japan, South Korea). No Latin American countries were on that list.

TIER 3: Countries on which the United States routinely spies but with whom it virtually never cooperates such as Venezuela, China, Iran, Venezuela and Syria. But the third tier also includes countries ranging from generally friendly to neutral countries such as: Brazil, Mexico, Argentina, Indonesia, South Africa, Kenya.

Finally, we now know of the following covert NSA operations:

EGOTISTICAL GIRAFFE: The NSA used known exploits in Firefox to target old versions of the Tor browser, an anonymity tool enabling Internet users to browse the net anonymously.

MUSCULAR: Launched in 2009, MUSCULAR infiltrates links between global data centers of technology companies such as Google and Yahoo not on US soil. These two companies have responded to MUSCULAR by encrypting these exchanges.

XKEYSCORE: The software interface through which NSA analysts search vast databases collected under various other operations. XKEYSCORE analyzes emails, online chats and the browsing histories of millions of individuals anywhere in the world. The XKEYSCORE data has been shared with other secret services including Australia's Defence Signals Directorate and New Zealand's Government Communications Security Bureau.

BULLRUN: Not in and of itself a surveillance program, BULLRUN is an operation by which the NSA undermines the security tools relied upon by users, targets, and non-targets. BULLRUN represents an apparently unprecedented effort to sabotage security tools in general use.

DISHFIRE: The Dishfire operation is the worldwide mass collection of text messages and other phone records, including location data, contact retrievals, credit card details, missed call alerts, roaming alerts (which indicate border crossings), electronic business cards, credit card payment notifications, travel itinerary alerts, meeting information, etc. Communications from US phones have been allegedly minimized, although not necessarily purged, from this database. The messages and associated data from non-US-persons were retained and analyzed.

CO-TRAVELER: Under this operation, the US collects location information from global cell towers, Wi-Fi, and GPS hubs. This information is collected and analyzed over time, in part in order to determine a target's traveling companions.

OLYMPIA: Canada's program to spy on the Brazilian Ministry of Mines and Energy.

BLARNEY: A program to leverage unique key corporate partnerships to gain access to high-capacity international fiber optic cables, switches and routers throughout the world. Countries targeted by Blarney include: Brazil, France, Germany, Greece, Israel, Italy, Japan, Mexico, South Korea, and Venezuela as well as the European Union and the United Nations.

and much more ....

While the Snowden revelations have proved invaluable in confirming the details of global, cross-border spying by the NSA (and its four primary allies), the governments of the affected billions of Internet and telephone users have been slow to fight back. In some cases, America's allies might be holding back because of their own tangled complicity in this shared network – or else, like Russia and China, they have their own pervasive surveillance networks and arrangements to protect.

But now that a year has passed it's clear that we need to update both our global technical infrastructure and local laws, consistent with long-standing international human rights standards, in order to regain any reasonable degree of privacy. Specifically, we must end mass surveillance. Politicians in every country need to stand up to the NSA's incursions on their territory; the United States needs to reform its laws to recognize the privacy rights of innocent foreigners, and the international community needs to set clear standards which makes any state conducting mass surveillance a pariah.

Clarification: We have edited this post to make it clear that much of what we've learned in the past year has been the specifics of how the NSA and its partners spy on ordinary people around the world. Our original post implied that we learned about that spying for the first time in the wake of the Snowden disclosures. Indeed, we have known for many years about the NSA and its partners' efforts to surveil the globe.

1. What did Edward Snowden's revelations about the NSA reveal about current privacy laws?

2. Should the United States reform its laws to recognize the privacy rights of foreign nationals?

"WHISTLEBLOWERS AND LEAK ACTIVISTS FACE POWERFUL ELITES IN STRUGGLE TO CONTROL INFORMATION," BY ARNE HINTZ, FROM *THE CONVERSATION*, APRIL 6, 2016

The Panama Papers have brought the powerful role of whistleblowers back into the public consciousness. Several years after WikiLeaks' Cablegate and the Snowden revelations, the next big leak has not only caused the downfall of Iceland's prime minister (with others possibly to follow), but has demonstrated that the practice of exposing hidden information is very much alive. The struggle over controlling this kind of information is one of the great conflicts of our times.

It might seem that such leaks are rare. WikiLeaks' publication in 2010 of the Iraq and Afghanistan war diaries and of US diplomatic cables brought major political repercussions, but public interest in WikiLeaks has fallen since. Whistleblower Edward Snowden's revelations in 2013 about mass surveillance programs by US and British intelligence services returned the power of the leak to the spotlight, triggering new legislation in the UK in the form of the Investigatory Powers Bill. But no mass movement of whistleblowers appears to have emerged in their wake.

Nevertheless, plenty has been going on. WikiLeaks has continued to expose hidden information, including files on Guantanamo Bay operations, secret drafts of the controversial TPP trade negotiations, and more recently a recording of an IMF meeting that provides significant insights into current conflicts between the IMF, the EU and the Greek government in their handling of the euro-zone crisis. Other leaks include those that revealed HSBC bank helped clients conceal their wealth.

Old-world and new-world media organizations have developed processes to deal with anonymous data leaks and protect the safety of the whistleblowers. Organizations such as the *New York Times, The Guardian* and *Al-Jazeera* use secure digital dropboxes for depositing files anonymously. Major publishers established collaborations to share resources and expertise in order to analyze and make sense of the huge amount of data quickly and to maximize international exposure.

LEAK ACTIVISM AND HACKTIVISM

And beyond the major news organizations, a culture of "leaks activism" has emerged. Hacktivist groups such as Globaleaks have developed technology for secure and anonymous leaking. Local or thematically-oriented initiatives provide new opportunities for whistleblowers to expose secret information. Citizen Leaks in Spain, for example, acts as an intermediary that accepts leaks, reviews them, and sends them on to partner newspapers. Run by Xnet, an anti-corruption group, Citizen Leaks has helped uncover major cases of corruption in Spain that brought to court leading Spanish politicians such as former minister of the economy and chairman of Spain's largest bank, Rodrigo Rato.

As intermediaries rather than publishers, organizations such as Citizen Leaks remain largely invisible to the public. But their role is crucial to expose corruption and other wrongdoings and so they are an important feature of the changing media landscape. Following the WikiLeaks revelations in 2010-11, US scholar Yochai Benkler conceptualized this emerging news environment as a "networked fourth estate", in which classic news organizations interact with citizen journalists, alternative and community media, online news platforms, and new organizations such as WikiLeaks and Citizen Leaks. In Snowden's case, he (the whistleblower) worked with documentary filmmaker Laura Poitras, independent journalist and former lawyer Glenn Greenwald, and *The Guardian*, a traditional media organization.

Leaks activist groups and platforms are increasingly relevant because digitization makes it easy to collect and transmit vast troves of data. The 7,000 pages of the Pentagon Papers that Daniel Ellsberg had to photocopy in 1971 would be a small PDF file today, while the huge amounts of documents that comprise the Panama Papers would have been impossible to leak in pre-digital times.

NO LOVE LOST FOR WHISTLEBLOWERS

Consequently, as organizations become more vulnerable to leaks they try to protect themselves through other means. The Insider Threat Program adopted for US public administrative agencies requires employees to report to their superiors any "suspicious" behavior by colleagues.

Under the Obama administration more whistleblowers have been prosecuted than under all previous Presidents combined. Chelsea Manning was sentenced to 35 years in prison, Julian Assange is holed up in the Ecuadorian Embassy in London, and Snowden lives in exile in Russia. So as leaks become more common, the response by states and corporations becomes harsher.

Whistleblowers are exposing the secrets of the powerful and the foundations on which contemporary political and economic power relations are built. Activism based around hacking, leaks and the release of data has put tools to affect world politics into the hands of those outside the classic structures of power and influence. Yet as previous high-profile leaks have shown, the degree and direction of change is far from clear, and there's no doubt that the consequences for whistleblowers can be life-changing. With the stakes rarely higher, the struggle to control information is likely to stay at the top of the political agenda.

1. What role do intermediary organizations like Citizen Leaks play in exposing corruption?

2. How has technology made it easier for people to become whistleblowers?

"RESPONSIBLE DATA LEAKS AND WHISTLEBLOWING," BY ALIX DUNN AND RUTH MILLER, FROM RESPONSIBLE DATA FORUM, OCTOBER 20, 2016

Large data breaches and leaks now regularly affect even the most seemingly well-guarded organizations and institutions. Over the past five years, a higher volume of data has been released to the public than the previous 50 years put together. This wave of leaks and breaches means that media outlets, the public, and political systems need to decide how best to serve the public interest when data is made available online.

This information can come from many sources:

A data breach is a compromise of security that leads to the accidental or unlawful destruction, loss, alteration, unauthorized disclosure of, or access to protected data. This is often (but not only) as the result of an attack from an outsider. Data dumps from breaches are becoming increasingly common. It can be difficult to distinguish between the two. Examples of data breaches that are assumed to be from outside attacks include things like DC Leaks and the leak of Democratic National Convention emails.

A data leak is a data breach where the source of the data is from someone inside the organization or institution that has collected that data. This usually takes the form of whistleblowing (the act of telling authorities or the public that someone else is doing something immoral or illegal). A government or private-sector employee who shares data with the public, or a group of individuals that shows that their employer is engaged in what they perceive to be malpractice. While whistleblowing has led to unprecedented exposure of secret and illegal government surveillance, corporate malfeasance and corruption, there is often little transparency about the decisions that determine when, how, and what data is released to the public.

As a result, there are serious responsible data issues to be grappled with. As with many responsible data grey areas, there are likely few hard and fast rules, but rather questions to be considered and addressed on a contextual basis.

Broadly speaking, responsible data practices for managing and publishing on data leaks from whistleblowers and other sources need to take the following points into consideration (this list is likely not exhaustive!):

- speedy, high quality publication of data leaks relevant to the public interest
- explicit communication about data provenance, governance, and quality taking care to protect sources when relevant
- appropriate planning for preservation and accessibility of large leaks, where relevant (the most obvious being well-organized repositories for preservation and search)
- operational security and residual data that can expose anonymous sources
- explicit principles for responsibly managing, publishing, reporting, and verifying data dumps
- whistleblower policies and media practices that create an enabling environment for whistleblowing and legal protections for whistleblowing

CARING FOR THE PEOPLE IN THE DATA

Data leaks and whistleblowing inherently requires sharing data without the consent of its creators or owners. In fact, in many cases, data owners are often the target of data leaks. However, owners of the data are unlikely to be the only people reflected in a dataset that hasn't been treated in advance.

Being incidentally included in a particular dataset can have damaging consequences. For example, this summer, Wikileaks published personally identifiable information of women in Turkey. They appear to have been included in what was thought to have been emails related to President Erdogan. As technosociologist and scholar Zeynep Tufekci wrote at the time, there were serious consequences of this release.

> "I hope that people remember this story when they report about a country without checking with anyone who speaks the language; when they support unaccountable, massive, unfiltered leaks without teaming up with responsible parties like journalists and ethical activists; and when they wonder why so many people around the world are wary of 'internet freedom' when it can mean indiscriminate victimization and senseless violations of privacy."

The responsible approach to dealing with this data would have been to work to verify the data prior to publishing it online, redacting it to ensure that no sensitive data was included, and establishing that the data was indeed an issue of public interest. Given the size and scale of the data, this is harder than it might sound. And in this case, it was made more difficult by language barriers and lack of adequate context to understand the contents of the leak, prior to it being made available online.

As with all responsible data issues – context is queen. In the case of data leaks, the diverse number of actors and incentives in the chain of data handling make understanding and decision-making in diverse contexts challenging.

DATA LEAKS AND WHISTLEBLOWING BEST PRACTICES

With the advent of high profile whistleblowers, much has been written and done to ensure the safety of those carrying out the act of whistleblowing, both in terms of behavioral best practices, legislative protections, and ensuring that technical best practices are possible via platforms like Secure Drop and GlobaLeaks.

But there are others who need to make important decisions about data leaks: publishers and consumers of the data.

Potential users might include journalists (those working within a newsroom, and freelancers), students, researchers, activists, academics, data scientists, and more. The field of journalism is established enough to have various codes of ethics, dependent upon the newsroom or the particular union, but as a younger field, data science lacks this, as identified by Nathaniel Poor in this case study contemplating the use of hacked data in academia:

> "Journalists use data and information in circumstances where authorities and significant portions of the public don't want the data released, such as with Wikileaks, and Edward Snowden... However, journalists also have robust professional norms and well-established ethics codes that the relatively young field of data science lacks. Although cases like Snowden are contentious, there is widespread acceptance that journalists have some responsibility to the public good which gives them latitude for professional judgment. Without that history, establishing a peer-group consensus and public goodwill about the right action in data science research is a challenge."

A number of efforts have been made to introduce ethics into data science curricula – which addresses part, but not all, of the problem. Not all of the potential users or even hosters of the data, will identify as a 'journalist' or a 'data scientist'. If data is made available through whistleblowing, perhaps different contextual considerations will apply, though lessons can definitely be learned from other, related sectors.

Calls have long been made for data journalists to consider their ethical responsibilities prior to publishing. Writing about the use of big data by academic researchers, Boyd and Crawford write: "it is unethical for researchers to justify their actions as ethical simply because the data is accessible."

This mantra might well apply to anyone who is thinking of using, or hosting, leaked data – so, what questions should they ask before using that data? Are there red lines that we should never cross, on both the side of the source and the data user – like data on individuals' bank account numbers, health status, sexual orientation, to name just a few. Might it be possible to agree upon a few, shared lines that don't get crossed, even in leaks?

Once someone decides to work with data made available through whistleblowing, what responsible data approaches can they take to ensure that no further harm comes to people reflected in that data set? This might involve taking steps to verify the data and making this process transparent, to ensure that others understand where it came from and what the data represents (and doesn't represent) – or redacting versions of a dataset before publishing it publicly.

TRANSPARENCY, PRIVACY AND PROTECTION

Looking at past examples, the approach of radical transparency rarely seems to be the most responsible approach for working with or dealing with data that has been made available through whistleblowing.

Alex Howard and John Wonderlich of the Sunlight Foundation write:

> "Weaponized transparency of private data of people in democratic institutions by unaccountable entities is destructive to our political norms, and to an open, discursive politics…. In every case, for every person described in the data, there's a public interest balancing test that includes foreseeable harms."

From a responsible data approach, those "foreseeable harms" are exactly what need to be outlined in advance and transparently considered. This might well end up being a controversial topic – as with many responsible data issues, things are rarely black and white.

The team behind the Panama Papers decided not to publish their original source documents, with ICIJ director Gerard Ryle quoted in *WIRED* as saying "We're not WikiLeaks. We're trying to show that journalism can be done responsibly." Discussion on the Responsible Data mailing list revealed multiple perspectives on the issue. Some thought that full transparency of the source documents would have been a better decision, while to others trusted that the team had responsibly taken the decision not to publish for a reason.

Ultimately, as Howard and Wonderlich also outline: protecting the privacy of individuals reflected in data that has been made available through whistleblowing should be of utmost importance.

TRUST AND RESPONSIBILITY

Ultimately, what underlines many of these concerns is trust. For the whistleblower releasing information, it is critical to ensure trust in a secure process of putting those leaks to use. It requires a great deal of faith to ask someone whose trust has been betrayed by an institution to then place it within journalists, researchers or activists who they might not personally know.

For a media outlet reporting on data leaks or data breaches of unknown provenance, responsibility is key. Beyond this, individuals need to think carefully about their responsibilities when using and accessing the data, and making it available for others to use in the future.

- What can we do as a community to encourage transparent, explicit communications around those decisions?
- To make it easier for a whistleblower to trust that transparent and responsible processes will be followed, with a duty of care towards both the public interest, and the rights of the people reflected in the data?
- What are ethical ways of reporting on data leaks whose provenance is unknown, or whose provenance is known to be from dubious actors using dubious tactics?
- How can media effectively make decisions and communicate those decisions to its consumers when reporting on data leaks and using them in their reporting?

To join in responsible data conversations on this topic and more, join us on the Responsible Data mailing list.

1. Why is radical transparency not always the best approach to data?

2. According to the author, what are some challenges to freedom of the press today?

CHAPTER 5

WHAT THE MEDIA SAY

The media plays a crucial role in whistleblowing. Good journalists hold themselves to a code of ethics that is clear and easy for their readers to understand. It is their role to determine and report on leaks that point out corruption and illegal activity while also holding back information that could put people in danger. The media can also offer protection to high-profile whistleblowers who fear retaliation, and help gain public support for the whistleblower and their cause. In cases of high-level corruption, the media might be a whistleblower's only uncompromised outlet for reporting. It is up to journalists to investigate and prove claims brought to them by whistleblowers before reporting. As legal cases against journalists who report on leaks begin to rise, reporters must take steps to protect themselves as well. The fear of legal trouble is a silencing tactic that many oppressive governments use to keep journalists from reporting leaks.

"10 WAYS MOVEMENTS CAN ENCOURAGE AND SUPPORT WHISTLEBLOWERS," BY ANTHONY KELLY, FROM WAGING NONVIOLENCE, MARCH 23, 2017

Whistleblowers from within institutions, corporations, government departments, police or military can be critical to movement success, and their testimony is often the key to exposing and resisting injustice and creating change.

Institutions clamp down on and deter whistleblowing for good reason. Whistleblowers can shake major institutions. They can feed vital information to movements, can warn activists about impending threats, can expose corruption, public health dangers and reduce the power of governments and deep state agencies. Disclosing secrets and releasing information poses high risks and personal costs and always takes a fair degree of courage. To expose an injustice, whistleblowers will have to trust who they are communicating with.

Nonviolent politics has long recognized that societal institutions, even rigid hierarchies such as the police or military, are not monolithic, but are in fact riddled with dissent. Institutions are made up of individual human beings. Despite well-developed cultural, legal and bureaucratic mechanisms used to enforce internal obedience and discipline, whistleblowing and other forms of internal resistance are surprisingly common.

So, what can activists, organizers and movements do to encourage and support whistleblowers?

1. DON'T ALIENATE THEM.

Avoid generalized public statements that are likely to deter whistleblowers from approaching you. Saying things like "All cops are bastards" or "Everyone who works for Exxon should be charged with crimes against humanity" are likely to dissuade potential whistleblowers from contacting you. If the activist group or movement is perceived to be hostile, violent, unorganized or antagonistic then being approached by a whistleblower is far less likely. Targeting critiques toward management, government leaders or the decision-makers and not ordinary workers or the rank and file makes an approach more likely.

2. SEND OUT INVITATIONS.

Publicly address and encourage people within the institution to blow the whistle on unjust or illegal practices. Talk about "people of conscience" within the institution. Actively and openly call upon people of courage and conviction within the ranks to tell their story. At rallies and public events engage with staff or rank-and-file workers to demonstrate that you are not hostile to them as individuals.

3. COMMUNICATE YOUR SUPPORT.

Use leaflets, speeches, union newsletters, social media and statements to the mainstream media to show that you or the movement can be trusted to support and protect whistleblowers. Let them know that you are open to hearing from them. Don't make promises you can't keep but offer support when and where you can.

4. CREATE AND PROMOTE AVENUES FOR INTERACTION.

Develop or utilize secure anonymous document drop links that you actively monitor. SecureDrop is one open-source whistleblower submission system that media organizations can use to securely accept documents from and communicate with anonymous sources. It was originally created by the late Aaron Swartz and is currently managed by Freedom of the Press Foundation.

Develop activities or events that encourage inter-action between the movement and staff. Organize a BBQ or dinner for staff, a public meeting for workers where they can hear about the movement. In Australia at Roxby Downs, anti-uranium activists held public meetings in the township to listen to the concerns of mine workers and their families. During the Vietnam War peace activists and veteran groups set up G.I. Coffee Houses near military bases. The principle is the same: Positive interaction generates trust and encourages internal dissent.

5. PRIORITIZE AND ACTIVELY ENGAGE WITH ANY CONTACTS.

Potential whistleblowers will often put out subtle "feelers" long before disclosing who they are or before releasing any information. They are seeking trusted contacts and testing you out. How activists respond to these initial contacts can be critical. Be open to communication that may appear suspicious at first or from dubious or anonymous sources. The general rule is to be respectful and courteous to all contacts as any one of them could end up being a critically important whistleblower.

6. ENSURE CONFIDENTIALITY.

If a potential whistleblower does make contact with you and identifies themselves in some way, make it a priority and do everything possible to ensure confidentiality. Drop other work if you need to in order to engage with them.

7. CONDUCT A RISK ASSESSMENT.

The risks for a whistleblower increase dramatically once they have made contact or gone public. Discuss with them what their fears and concerns are and help them conduct a risk assessment, which is essentially listing, discussing and then evaluating each identified risk. Seek out legal support for them that is capable of advising and advocating for them in the case of legal sanctions. Whistleblowers may be breaking contracts, agreements, regulations and laws in order to make information public. Form a small and capable support team around the whistleblower.

The decision to go to the media needs to be considered carefully and the whistleblower should be supported to make the best and safest decision for them as they will bear the vast bulk of any consequences. Having a high profile in the media can be a risk but can also lead to additional safety.

If the decision is made to go to the media, choose the most experienced journalist in the most reputable media outlet available. Take the time to find the right one. Professional journalists who adhere to professional ethics should protect sources and may be able to work with you on making information go public safely. But not all journalists will act ethically and will also have their own interests in breaking a story. You can act as a go-between at the early stages to reduce the risks for the whistleblower.

8. SHARE RESOURCES FOR WHISTLEBLOWERS

Provide them with a copy of "The Whistleblower's Handbook: How to Be an Effective Resister" by Brian Martin. It is out of print but available online. Based upon hundreds of interviews with whistleblowers, this book provides insights, lessons and important advice for people considering blowing the whistle in the public interest.

9. BE READY TO PROVIDE PROTECTION.

Work with your networks or activist group to provide as much support, security or protection as possible. In some cases this may mean making sure someone trusted is with them 24 hours a day for a while. This form of "protective accompaniment" would mean creating a roster to have trusted people stay with the person and a protocol to alert more support if there is a threat or incident.

10. PREPARE TO GIVE ONGOING SUPPORT.

Whistleblowers are often risking their safety, careers, incomes and reputations when deciding to release information on corruption or injustice. They will face damaging personal attacks and harassment, traumatic and long legal battles and possibly imprisonment. They deserve the ongoing and long-term support of the movement. Some movements have set up ongoing support groups for whistleblowers that raise funds and generate public and political support.

The Chelsea Manning Support Network operated for seven years and was able to cover 100 percent of Chelsea Manning's legal fees throughout her court martial — nearly $400,000 — and mount a huge publicity campaign to raise awareness about her situation. Other groups like the Courage Foundation support several "truth-tellers" internationally, and fundraise for the legal and public defense of specific individuals who risk life or liberty to make significant contributions to the historical record and are subject to serious prosecution or persecution. The more support existing whistleblowers receive, the more likely others will follow.

Whistleblowing poses a serious threat to power, privilege and the continuation of anti-democratic or authoritarian practices. Our movements grow stronger when we support them. Every bit of encouragement, support and protection you can provide is worth it.

1. What should a whistleblower consider before going to the media?

2. What kind of support do whistleblowers need?

"WHY COMPANIES LIKE WELLS FARGO IGNORE THEIR WHISTLEBLOWERS – AT THEIR PERIL," BY ELIZABETH C. TIPPETT, FROM *THE CONVERSATION*, OCTOBER 24, 2017

Enron. Worldcom. The Madoff scandal. The mortgage meltdown. Now Wells Fargo.

High-profile corporate frauds like these all seem to follow the same pattern. First the misconduct is discovered, and then we learn about all of the whistleblowers who tried to stop the fraud much earlier. Congress then tries to enhance whistleblower protections, with varying success.

The Sarbanes-Oxley Act, passed in 2002 after the Enron and Worlcom scandals, was supposed to protect whistleblowers who uncovered accounting frauds, but judges typically rejected their retaliation claims. The Dodd Frank Act, approved in 2010, provides financial rewards for certain whistleblowers. Its success is still unclear.

While these laws may protect employees who expose wrongdoing from retaliation and encourage more to do the same, nothing requires employers to take their disclosures seriously. And as we saw with the latest scandal involving Wells Fargo, several former employees say they tried to get the company's attention in 2005 and 2006, to no avail.

Their ineffectiveness is hardly unique. The 2011 National Business Ethics Survey found that 40 percent of employees who reported misconduct believed that their report had not been investigated. When an investigation did take place, over half thought the process was unfair.

So why don't companies make better use of the information they get from their whistleblowers – especially when ignoring them could expose their company to millions or even billions in liability and permanently tarnish their brand?

WHO LOOKS THE PART

For a start, real whistleblowers don't always match our mental image.

Our idealized image of whistleblowers isn't doing us any favors. We assume that whistleblowing will come from top employees. But when the company already has a poor ethics culture, those top employees may very well be the ones engaged in the misconduct.

Instead, as I described in a previous research paper, important information might originate from employees who don't fit in or are labeled as complainers or poor performers.

In other words, we expect the true whistleblower to be Ryan Gosling's suave character in "The Big Short," while ignoring the angry insights from Steve Carrell, on account of his bad haircut and terrible social skills.

To take whistleblowers seriously, we need to set aside our judgments about them and their motives and focus instead on the message they convey. In the words of negotiation gurus Roger Fisher and Bill Ury, "separate the people from the problem."

WHERE THERE'S SMOKE, IS THERE FIRE?

A second problem with whistleblowing is that we tend to assume it's not an emergency if other people don't think so.

There is a principle in social psychology known as the "bystander effect," which essentially means that people defer to others on how to interpret ambiguous situations and dread the idea of overreacting to a situation and later being embarrassed. It also means that when you observe others doing nothing in response to an apparent risk, you're more likely to do the same.

In a famous experiment, researchers observed how people reacted to a room filling with smoke, contrasting the behavior of those who were alone to those accompanied by others who were instructed in advance to appear indifferent to the smoke. Of those who were alone, 75 percent reported the smoke to the experimenter. By contrast, only 10 percent of the subjects sitting with the passive seatmates reported the smoke.

The same may be true of whistleblowing. The fact that "everyone knows" about a particular type of misconduct may actually make people less likely to report it. In addition, when a particular type of misconduct becomes prevalent, those investigating may discount the severity of conduct they see frequently and thereby fail to realize that it has reached a crisis level.

HOW WHISTLEBLOWING IS LIKE AN ICEBERG

Another problem is that whistleblowers may not know which information is most important.

Whistleblowers, especially those uncovering substantial misconduct, have only one piece of what might be a much larger puzzle. They also aren't lawyers, so they don't know whether a piece of information is legally important. They only know that the situation feels wrong. Consequently, the important nugget of information might be buried within a lot of irrelevant information.

The 2006 letter from a Wells Fargo whistleblower – who disclosed that other employees were opening fake accounts – is a good example of this problem. The first page of the letter contains generic complaints about unfair treatment and possibly age discrimination. The second page then talks about how salespeople "gamed" the system to inflate their sales numbers – but apparently with the assistance and consent of the customer involved. Sandwiched between these (somewhat) benign accusations is a story about how a customer complained that accounts were opened without his knowledge or consent.

Wells Fargo apparently ignored the report, to its peril and the detriment of millions of customers. The person reading the letter may have started out feeling suspicious of the whistleblower, confirmed that suspicion based on the first page of the letter and then completely missed the important information on the second page. Like this illusion, once the reader forms an initial impression (e.g., that the image features a duck), they became blind to additional data that contradicts the impression (the image could also be a rabbit).

The idea that we "see what we want to see" is not mere conjecture. One study found that people literally saw what they wanted to see in a drawing, perceiving an ambiguous drawing as a "B" or the number "13" depending upon which interpretation led to a more favorable result for themselves in the experiment.

CHALLENGES INVESTIGATING COMPLAINTS

And a final problem: Explosive complaints are as rare as explosive luggage.

Publicly traded companies like Wells Fargo are required under Sarbanes-Oxley to have a process for receiving and responding to anonymous whistleblower complaints. Wells Fargo, like many other companies, had a whistleblower hotline. Why didn't those folks — whose job it was to investigate complaints — uncover the misconduct early enough to stop it?

Investigating corporate complaints is a lot like being a Transportation Security Administration agent. Most of the complaints they are sorting through will be regular luggage, with a few unauthorized bottles of liquid here and there. Take the problem of reading that 2006 letter and multiply it by 100 or 1,000 letters, almost all of which describe an isolated problem or conduct that isn't illegal. You don't get much practice at the most important part of your job (identifying explosives) when it virtually never happens.

Like TSA agents, investigators also have the challenge of identifying a new form of misconduct that doesn't match the mental models of prior bad acts. In other words, Wells Fargo may have been most worried about mortgage fraud when they should have spent more time investigating fraud in retail banking.

Great investigators are like the guys from the History Channel's "American Pickers" show. They meet the owners, listen to their story, go through the stuff themselves and then make judgments about what to pursue based on their independent judgment and experience. They're also open to finding the "best" stuff in unexpected places.

Lastly, great investigators keep an eye out for patterns, noticing when seemingly isolated incidents may indicate a larger problem.

AN INVALUABLE ASSET

Managers and corporate officers responding to complaints need to shed their preconceptions about whistleblowers and instead invest in the information they receive.

Rather than grumbling about the cost of dealing with them, companies should view their information as a valuable corporate asset. Preventative investments like training managers on responding to whistleblowers, maintaining a hotline and hiring investigators and compliance officers to follow their leads ultimately serve a company's long-term interests.

If the Wells Fargo scandal proves anything, it is that a 164-year-old brand can be tarnished overnight. A whistleblower – however flawed she may be – may be the last person standing between a company and the loss of its reputation.

1. How does the "bystander effect" work on potential whistleblowers?

2. What should whistleblowers do if they feel their complaint is being ignored?

"WHY TRUMP'S WHITE HOUSE LEAKS," BY FREDERIC LEMIEUX, FROM *THE CONVERSATION*, MAY 16, 2017

According to the *Washington Post*, President Donald Trump revealed highly classified information to the Russian Foreign Minister Sergey Lavrov and members of his delegation during a May 10 meeting in the Oval Office.

In a May 15 story, the *Post* reported that White House staffers tried to contain the damage by striking Trump's allegedly inappropriate comments from internal memos.

So how did the *Washington Post* get the story?

The newspaper story cites "current and former U.S. officials" as sources. Later, the reporters offer more detail, describing one source as "a former senior U.S. counter-terrorism official who also worked closely with members of the Trump national security team."

Translation: The public learned of Trump's apparent overstep because more than one member of the U.S. intelligence community was willing to leak the information.

Professor of the practice and faculty director of the master's in applied intelligence at Georgetown University, I study, teach and write about homeland security and law enforcement intelligence. I'm curious about why intelligence officers disclose classified information and how that affects their work.

WHY WHISPERS START

Leakers and whistleblowers often are motivated by a lack of trust in their chain of command. They denounce wrongdoing and express their dissent through leaking information to the media or advocacy groups. In my view, one example of wrongdoing that is particularly salient today is political interference in intelligence activities.

Trust is undermined when the gathering or sharing of intelligence influences politics or is influenced by politics.

Bottom-up politicization happens when members of the intelligence agencies themselves target individuals or issues for political reasons. For instance, intelligence agencies may go after political opponents to maintain or increase the level of influence they enjoy with the government.

J. Edgar Hoover was renowned for using the resources of the FBI to interfere in politics and keep his job as the head of the FBI for 48 years.

Top-down politicization happens when policymakers – all the way up to the president – spin intelligence and investigations to support their political agenda. A famous case study is the 2002 national intelligence estimate on weapons of mass destruction in Iraq. Then-Vice President Dick Cheney reportedly pressured CIA analysts to quickly produce a report confirming the existence of WMD. Although the evidence was rather tepid, Cheney and George W. Bush used that intelligence to justify the U.S. invasion of Iraq.

Another famous example of top-down politicization comes from President Richard Nixon, who obstructed the special investigation in the Watergate scandal.

PLENTY OF BAD BLOOD

How does this relate to Trump's most recent meeting with Lavrov?

This latest political drama happened in the midst of a high-profile investigation regarding possible collusion between the Trump campaign staff and the Russian government. And it comes just a week after the dismissal of FBI Director James Comey escalated the tension between the White House and intelligence agencies.

The firing of Comey rattled the FBI, spurring some agency employees to express anonymously their intention to wage a "concerted effort to respond over time in kind."

But the bad blood goes back even further. In February, Trump accused the FBI of leaking information about the Russian investigation. And, in March, the president expressed his belief that Trump Tower was wiretapped by former President Obama with the help of the Department of Justice.

Hostility between Trump and the intelligence agencies has been heightened by a series of decisions by the White House.

First, on Jan. 31, 2017, Trump fired Sally Yates, acting attorney general, after she informed the White House several times that then National Security Advisor Michael Flynn had lied about his contacts with Russians.

Then, Attorney General Jeff Sessions recused himself from any investigation related to the Russia meddling with the 2016 presidential elections because he omitted to disclose two meetings with the Russian ambassador.

In addition, Rep. Devin Nunes, the chairman of the House Intelligence Committee, had to recuse himself from the investigation on Russian interference in the 2016 election because he was being investigated by the House Committee on Ethics for making unauthorized disclosures of classified information.

Finally, Comey was dismissed a few days after he requested more resources to accelerate the probe on Russia's interference in the election.

These events undermine the perception of integrity of the investigative process – not just by the general public, but by intelligence officers and investigators. In this environment, it should be expected that more classified information will be disclosed and whistleblowers will come forward. And, there's a real possibility of an intensified political tug of war in which leakers and whistleblowers deliberately undermine the White House while President Trump tries to do the same to the Russian investigation.

INTELLIGENCE WHISTLEBLOWERS

SIXTEEN OF THE MOST WELL-KNOWN AND IMPACTFUL SNITCHES IN RECENT U.S. HISTORY

NAME & ORGANIZATION	YEAR	ACTION	CONSEQUENCES
Daniel Ellsberg, U.S. Department of State	1971	Released the Pentagon Papers and unveiled a series of public deceptions by the U.S. government regarding the Vietnam War.	Legal action taken in Supreme Court against the U.S. government's action to hide classified information regarding the conduct of the war.
Perry Fellwock, National Security Agency	1971	NSA analyst who disclosed the existence of the secret agency and its global surveillance activities.	The revelations triggered the work of the Church Commission and the establishment of rules against domestic interception of communications
Mark Felt, also known as "Deep Throat," Federal Bureau of Investigation	1972	Associate director of the FBI, he revealed the involvement of President Nixon in the Watergate scandal.	Under threat of impeachment, Nixon resigned as president
Frank Snepp, Central Intelligence Agency	1977	CIA analyst who revealed the poor degree of preparation of the U.S. military in anticipating the fall of Saigon.	Snepp was successfully prosecuted for violation of his non-disclosure agreement and stripped of all his retirement benefits and book royalties.
Frederick Whitehurst, Federal Bureau of Investigation	1997	Forensic analyst at the FBI who disclosed the obsolete laboratory techniques for explosive analysis. He exposed several issues with World Trade Center (1993) and Oklahoma City bombings (1995), undermining the investigations.	His revelations provoked an entire modernization of the explosive forensic laboratories in the United States.

TABLE CONTINUED

NAME & ORGANIZATION	YEAR	ACTION	CONSEQUENCES
Coleen Rowley, Federal Bureau of Investigation	2002	FBI special agent who denounced the lack of foresight of the Bureau and the mishandling of critical intelligence related to 9/11.	Rowley was named person of the year by *Time* magazine for her revelations.
William Binney, J. Kirke Wiebe and Edward Loomis, National Security Agency	2002	Three NSA officials who informed the House Select Intelligence Committee about the financial waste and illegal eavesdropping of the NSA in the program called Trailblazer	The Inspector General of the Department of Defense concluded that Trailblazer project was ineffective and too expensive. The program was discontinued.
Sibel Edmonds, Federal Bureau of Investigation	2002	FBI translator who accused colleagues of covering up illicit activity involving Turkish nationals, alleged serious security breaches and cover-ups and that intelligence had been deliberately suppressed, endangering national security.	She was fired by the FBI and founded the National Security Whistleblowers Coalition in 2004.
Joseph Wilson, U.S. government	2003	Former diplomat who denounced the exaggeration of the nuclear threat posed by the regime of Saddam Hussein.	The Bush administration allegedly retaliated for the disclosure by leaking the identity of Wilson's wife (Valerie Plame), a CIA officer.
Samuel Provance, U.S. Army	2004	Former U.S. Army Intelligence sergeant who revealed the interrogation abuses at the Abu Ghraib prison.	The disclosure triggered a congressional investigation that led to the resignation of the Secretary of the Department of Defense Donald Rumsfeld.

NAME & ORGANIZATION	YEAR	ACTION	CONSEQUENCES
Russ Tice, National Security Agency	2005	One of the First NSA intelligence officer to denounce the constitutional violation perpetrated by the agency throughout warrantless surveillance programs.	No immediate impact on NSA activities but he became the first of a series of whistleblower denouncing the surveillance program of the agency.
Thomas A. Drake, National Security Agency	2005	NSA analyst who denounced the illegal surveillance program Trailblazer, which was violating the 4th amendment.	Indicted in 2010 for his revelations, the U.S. government dropped all charge in exchange for a guilty plea to a misdemeanor.
John Kiriakou, Central Intelligence Agency	2007	CIA officer who disclosed publicly the existence of waterboarding techniques on detainees.	He was sentenced to 30 months of imprisonment after giving to the media the name of a covert CIA operative who could corroborate his revelations about torture techniques.
Chelsea Manning, U.S. Army	2010	Army intelligence analyst who leaked publicly a large number of classified digital documents related to the Afghan and Iraqi wars.	Manning was convicted under the Espionage Act and convicted to 35 years of prison. The Obama administration commuted Manning's sentence in 2017.
Edward Snowden, Booz Allen Hamilton	2013	Contractor analyst who disclosed top-secret documents about mass surveillance programs managed by the National Security Agency.	Snowden fled to Russia to avoid being arrested and charges by the U.S. government. The disclosure of mass surveillance document provoked a political and media storm leading to interruption of bulk collection of metadata by Congress.
Sally Yates, Acting Attorney General	2017	Warned the Trump White House that National Security Advisor Michael Flynn had lied about his contacts with Russians, making him vulnerable to blackmail.	Yates was fired by Trump.

1. What might one motivation be for those who blow the whistle on their leaders?

"FROM THE PENTAGON PAPERS TO TRUMP: HOW THE GOVERNMENT GAINED THE UPPER HAND AGAINST LEAKERS," BY MARGOT SUSCA, FROM *THE CONVERSATION*, JUNE 15, 2017

In October 1969, a national security official named Daniel Ellsberg began secretly photocopying 7,000 classified Vietnam War documents. He had become increasingly frustrated with the systematic deception of top U.S. leaders who sought to publicly escalate a war that, privately, they knew was unwinnable.

In March 1971 he leaked the documents – what would became known as the Pentagon Papers – to a *New York Times* reporter. The newspaper ended up publishing a series of articles that exposed tactical and policy missteps by three administrations on a range of subjects, from covert operations to confusion over troop deployments.

In the decades since, the Pentagon Papers helped shape legal and ethical standards for journalistic truth-telling on matters of top secret government affairs in the United States. Openness, in the eyes of the public and the courts, would usually prevail over government secrecy. In this sense, the transparency that came from the papers' release shifted power from politicians back to citizens and news organizations.

That balance of power is taking on a renewed significance today. In the wake of Reality Winner's alleged recent national security leak, prosecution of members of the press over the past few years as well as pointed anti-press and anti-leak rhetoric by the Trump administration, one must ask: Are we witnessing a swing back toward strengthened government control of information?

POLITICAL LIES EXPOSED

The Pentagon Papers helped Americans realize that government officials didn't have qualms lying about policy. Perhaps more importantly, it showed them that the news media could act as a key conduit between the country's most powerful political elites and a public they meant to keep in the dark.

"They made people understand that presidents lie all the time, not just occasionally, but all the time. Not everything they say is a lie, but anything they say could be a lie," Ellsberg later said.

The New York Times began publishing the Pentagon Papers in June 1971. Citing national security concerns, the Nixon administration sought to stop publication of the papers. The case went all the way to the U.S. Supreme Court, where, in a landmark 6-3 ruling, *The New York Times* and *The Washington Post* won the right to continue publishing information contained in the documents.

AN UNSPOKEN BARGAIN

From the Pentagon Papers until the Obama administration, there was "an unspoken bargain of mutual restraint" between the press and the government, according to legal scholars David McCraw and Stephen Gikow. The press would occasionally publish classified information, and the executive branches would treat those leaks as a normal part of politics.

Veteran investigative reporter Dana Priest described such a relationship as giving reporters "a greater responsibility to be thoughtful about what it publishes and to give government the chance to make its case."

But since 2009, the federal government has grown increasingly hostile toward leakers and news organizations that have published classified information. As *The New York Times* noted in its coverage of Winner, President Trump, "like his predecessor Barack Obama, has signaled a willingness to pursue and prosecute government leakers."

During Obama's tenure, his administration prosecuted more leaks than every prior administration combined. He also continued to pursue high-profile cases against reporters who published stories using classified information. James Risen, a veteran national security reporter at *The New York Times* and target of such a case, called the Obama administration "the greatest enemy of press freedom in a generation."

TENSIONS MOUNT

So what happened? How did this "unspoken bargain" fall apart?

Technology has certainly created more tension between the government and media outlets. Government employees and contractors can electronically access and release information to websites like WikiLeaks, which, in turn, can instantly publicize tens of thousands of pages of classified records.

Mainstream news organizations are also experimenting with new ways for leakers to submit classified information. The Tow Center for Digital Journalism at the Columbia University Graduate School of Journalism created a guide for news organizations using SecureDrop, described as an "in-house system for news organizations to securely communicate with anonymous sources and receive documents over the Internet." ProPublica offers information on its website about how to leak "to hold people and institutions accountable."

In a sense, this is part of a continuing battle between the seemingly incompatible traditions of a free press and a national security apparatus that benefits from secrecy.

Government transparency is a necessary ingredient for a democracy. To elect leaders, citizens at the local, state and federal level need to have as much access to accurate information about policy and policymakers as possible. On the other hand, when it comes to national security, complete transparency could mean compromising information that puts lives at risks.

However, according to University of Minnesota law professor Heidi Kitrosser, the threats that leaks pose to national security are often exaggerated by a political system that benefits from a public that's kept in the dark about its leaders' actions. Kitrosser wrote that in one warrant filed during the Obama administration, a member of the press was labeled as "an alleged leaker's criminal coconspirator."

A WARY PUBLIC

Meanwhile, even though it's become easier to leak information – and for news outlets to expose government corruption and misdeeds – the public has become increasingly wary about leaks.

A 2007 Pew Research Center report found nearly 60 percent of Americans felt the U.S. government criticized news stories about national security because it had something to hide. That same study showed 42 percent of Americans thought leaks harmed the public interest. By 2013, 55 percent of Americans believed Edward Snowden's leaks about National Security Agency surveillance programs did more harm than good.

Such a dramatic change in public opinion raises questions about whether the public today will even defend the media's right to access and publish leaked information.

It certainly hasn't helped that, during the first year of the Trump administration, the press has been attacked ad nauseam. The president routinely calls news organizations "fake news" and threatens increased prosecution of leaks.

The rhetoric comes at a time when the public has expressed a growing disdain for journalism. A September 2016 Gallup poll revealed Americans' trust in the news media to "report the news fully, accurately and fairly" dropped to its lowest level since the group began asking the question in 1972.

LEAKING AND THE LAW

Public opinion on this issue matters because there are flimsy legal protections for journalists and leakers. And if politicians realize they can go after journalists without facing a backlash at the voting booth, they could become emboldened.

Because of Winner's leak, there are new questions about how much Russia interfered with the 2016 election. *The Intercept,* which published the document, called it "the most detailed U.S. government account of Russian interference in the election that has yet come to light."

Nonetheless, Winner now faces 10 years in prison. There hasn't been any legal action against the *Intercept,* perhaps because the government was able to track down Winner on its own.

Meanwhile, there's no federal shield law – also known as reporter's privilege – for journalists. Such a law would give journalists the legal right to protect the identities of confidential sources. However, 49 states and the District of Columbia offer some variation on reporter's privilege through either case law or statute.

In 2009, a federal shield law to protect journalists from testifying against their sources made its way onto the agenda. With bipartisan support and a Democratic Congress, Obama said he would refuse to sign the bill if it didn't include a significant exemption for national security. The bill went nowhere.

In 2008, law professor RonNell Andersen Jones studied 761 news organizations and found that reporters or editors in 2006 received 3,062 subpoenas "seeking information or material relating to newsgathering" – a number that, Andersen argued, justified federal legislation to protect them. Without firm legal protections, journalists face a lengthy – and potentially expensive – fight to fend off the government.

As journalism observers and researchers like me study how leaks, prosecutions and anti-media rhetoric impact everything from media trust to the free flow of information, we may be entering a post-Pentagon Papers era that shifts the power back to political elites, who seem more emboldened to go after leakers.

That's not good for the average citizen. Ellsberg knew it in 1969. We should pay more attention now, too.

1. How does anti-media rhetoric discourage whistleblowers?

2. Why has the public become wary of leaks?

"HOW SHOULD YOU READ UNNAMED SOURCES AND LEAKS?," BY ANTHONY FARGO, FROM *THE CONVERSATION*, JANUARY 23, 2017

During my 13-year career in professional journalism, I rarely encountered issues with confidential sources or leaks directly. But during graduate school I became fascinated by the legal complications of journalists protecting sources and have written about the right to speak anonymously for nearly 20 years.

Using unnamed sources and leaked information is fraught with ethical and legal perils for journalists, their employers and their sources. Whether the risks are worth it depends upon the importance of the story. But in an age when the term "fake news" is becoming part of the lexicon, how should readers judge the credibility of a story whose sources aren't revealed?

THE MINEFIELD OF UNNAMED SOURCES

Some selfless sources approach journalists in order to right a wrong or blow the whistle on a governmental or corporate betrayal of the public's trust. But sources also sometimes have axes to grind. This doesn't necessarily invalidate their information. However, it does mean that reporters must exercise caution when accepting their help, promising confidentiality or reporting on leaked documents.

The issue of sources came up recently when the media reported that a former British intelligence officer named Christopher Steele had written a dossier containing unconfirmed claims that Russia had compromising information about Donald Trump.

People who know Steele have spoken highly of his expertise and skill in gathering intelligence. But we have no way of judging whether his sources were reliable because we do not know who they were. The report had also been commissioned by Trump's opponents from both political parties. These circumstances create opportunities to discredit the leaked report.

The Code of Ethics for the Society of Professional Journalists reflects the messy relationship between sources and journalists. It instructs journalists to "identify sources clearly," "[c]onsider sources' motives before promising anonymity" and grant anonymity only to sources who would face harm if identified. The code also states that journalists should be "cautious when making promises, but keep the promises they make."

There's probably a reason the code suggests using anonymous sources only when absolutely necessary. Studies have shown that using unnamed sources hurts journalists' credibility with the public. At the same time, some potentially important stories would not be reported if journalists were unable to promise sources anonymity.

Famous examples of stories that relied to some extent on confidential sources include the Watergate scandal uncovered by *Washington Post* reporters Bob Woodward and Carl Bernstein that led to President Richard Nixon's resignation. The world's most famous anonymous source, "Deep Throat" (later revealed to be FBI Deputy Director Mark Felt), was only one of many confidential sources the reporters used.

Other examples are the Post's revelation that the United States was shipping post-9/11 detainees to secret prisons overseas where they could be questioned more "aggressively" and the exposure of the Catholic Church sex abuse scandal by the Boston Globe's Spotlight Team.

But there also have been instances when journalists have regretted relying on confidential sources, including the media's systemic failure to question the Bush administration's leaks about Saddam Hussein's alleged stockpile of weapons of mass destruction. Another example is the 2004 CBS Evening News story about President Bush's service in the Texas National Guard in the 1970s. Dan Rather retired early from his anchor chair after sources failed to defend the authenticity of documents critical of Bush's service.

AN OUTLET'S REPUTATION IS CRITICAL

All of this makes it difficult for readers to know whether to trust reports based on unnamed sources and leaks. The task for readers is further complicated by the explosion of new online media outlets that might not adhere to mainstream journalistic standards or best practices.

There are a few things readers should look for when determining whether to trust (or post or retweet) a story based on unnamed sources. First, the more specific the identification of the source and her reason for wanting her identity concealed, the better. For example, "A source with direct knowledge of the situation who did not want to be identified because she was not authorized to speak to the media" is better than "some people say."

Second, is the news outlet transparent about how it handles unnamed sources and sensitive documents? Many reputable sites are not but should be. Some news outlets have public editors or media critics who explain how news was gathered or criticize their own publications when they stray from best practices. Some also publish explainer pieces about how they gathered information about particularly controversial stories.

Finally, readers should remember that the media love controversy and conflict. Therefore, if a news site or channel delivers a vaguely sourced big scoop and no other media pick it up, readers should be very wary, particularly if the site is obscure or openly partisan.

FLIMSY LEGAL PROTECTIONS

While it's understandable that readers would be suspicious of stories that rely on unnamed sources – particularly if the sources have leaked classified information – they have good reason to ask journalists to protect their identities. In the wake of the Trump dossier's publication, Christopher Steele probably didn't flee his home to simply escape nosy reporters. He probably feared some sort of retaliation.

In the United States, sources who leak classified documents to journalists face possible prison time if their identities are exposed. Many are probably familiar with the leaks about National Security Agency eavesdropping by Edward Snowden (now self-exiled in Russia) and war-related documents by Chelsea Manning, who spent seven years in prison before President Obama commuted her sentence earlier this month.

While Obama might receive praise in some circles for this act, his Justice Department prosecuted at least twice as many people for leaking information as all previous administrations combined.

Journalists put themselves on the line too as their legal right to conceal the identities of their sources isn't well-established. According to the Reporters Committee for Freedom of the Press, at least 20 U.S. journalists have been jailed since 1972 for refusing to reveal sources. Many more have been fined.

In 1972, the U.S. Supreme Court ruled in Branzburg v. Hayes that the First Amendment didn't give journalists the right to not cooperate with grand juries, even if cooperation meant identifying sources. A concurring opinion by Justice Lewis Powell limited the 5-4 ruling to the particular cases involved, however, and federal courts ever since have tried to figure out what that means.

Thirty-nine states and the District of Columbia have shield laws that protect journalists from being forced to reveal sources to state and local authorities. But Congress' last attempt to pass a federal shield law in 2014 failed over concerns about whom the law would apply to, such as nonprofessional bloggers or sites like Wikileaks.

The legal problems of journalists and sources could be ameliorated by a strong, broad federal shield law, amendments to whistleblower laws to protect those who go public with concerns and a less aggressive use of the Espionage Act, which was used in the prosecution of Chelsea Manning.

In the end, the relationships between journalists and sources come down to trust. Sources must trust that journalists will protect their identities. Journalists must trust that sources are being truthful regardless of any ulterior motives. Readers, meanwhile, have to choose whether to trust media reports based on unnamed sources. Each reader has his or her own reasons for trusting or not trusting the news, but media outlets could help by relying as little as possible on unnamed sources and being as transparent as possible when they do.

With a president who has shown particular hostility to the press entering the White House, the media may have to rely more on unnamed sources and leaks to inform audiences.

Audiences, then, will have to decide where to place their trust: in the administration or in the media.

1. What things should readers look for when deciding whether or not to trust a report with an unnamed source?

2. How can journalists gain readers' trust when using unnamed sources?

"IS PART OF CHELSEA MANNING'S LEGACY INCREASED SURVEILLANCE?," BY SANJAY GOEL, FROM *THE CONVERSATION*, JANUARY 20, 2017

The military's most prolific leaker of digital documents has ushered in an age of even more increased surveillance over government workers. The legacy of Chelsea Manning's actions is under discussion in the wake of the announcement that the former Army private will be released from military prison in May. In one of his last official acts, President Obama commuted her sentence for violations of the Espionage Act and copying and disseminating classified information. The commutation reduced her sentence from 35 years to the seven years she has already served, plus four additional months needed to effect her release.

In 2010, Manning, then presenting as male and going by the first name Bradley, was an intelligence analyst serving in Iraq. Disillusioned by callous behavior and indiscriminate killing of people in Afghanistan and Iraq by American soldiers, Manning copied and digitally released a massive trove of classified information. The data included 250,000 cables from American diplomats stationed around the world, 470,000 Iraq and Afghanistan battlefield reports and logs of military incident reports, assessment files of detainees held at Guantanamo Bay and war zone videos of airstrikes in Afghanistan and Iraq war in which civilians were killed.

Government officials immediately expressed concerns about damage to national security, international relations and military personnel because of the information contained in the material. There appears to have been relatively little lasting damage to American diplomacy. The military revelations were more damaging, with documents discussing prisoner torture and an assassination squad made up of American special forces operators. Those enraged American citizens and the international community alike, and may have hardened the resolve of adversaries.

But the most lasting effect will likely be a powerful new fear of so-called "insider threats" – leaks by people like Manning, working for the U.S. and having passed security clearance background checks. In the wake of Manning's actions, the military and intelligence communities have been ramping up digital surveillance of their own personnel to unprecedented levels, in hopes of detecting leakers before they let their information loose on the world.

EMBARRASSING TO DIPLOMATS

The initial official response was that the release of State Department cables – internal communications between officials with candid assessments of international situations and even individual leaders' personalities –

would be so debilitating to foreign relations that repair would take decades.

In reality, the cables were more embarrassing than destructive. A political uproar met the news that the U.S. and its purported ally Pakistan were working at cross-purposes: American forces were trying to fight against the Taliban and al-Qaida, while Pakistan was trying to offer them protection and even weapons. But overall, it didn't significantly increase the existing tensions in American-Pakistani relations. Other foreign officials may have become more wary about sharing information with Americans, but over time, new people come into key posts, the leak is forgotten and business continues as it has always done.

Foreign leaders about whom U.S. officials had made blunt and disparaging comments in the cables did suffer. For example, the cables revealed a secret agreement in which the U.S. conducted drone strikes in Yemen while that country's President Ali Abdullah Saleh publicly took the blame. Two years later, in 2012, a popular revolution ousted him. A similar fate befell the Tunisian President Zine El Abidine Ben Ali, whose lavish lifestyle – and lack of American support – was discussed in the cables.

REVEALING MILITARY MISDEEDS

More damaging to the U.S. was what was revealed in the battlefield reports Manning released, and called evidence of American soldiers' "bloodlust." For instance, Manning's leaks disclosed the activities of an American assassination squad in Afghanistan. Called Task Force 373, the unit comprised specially trained U.S. personnel from elite forces such as the Navy SEALs and the Army's Delta Force. Its goal was to assassinate a range of targets including drug barons, drug makers and al-Qaida and Taliban figures.

The documents also showed U.S. military personnel shooting innocent civilians on the ground and from the air – among them a Reuters journalist. They showed that American authorities ignored extreme torture inflicted on Iraqi prisoners, including sexual abuse and physical mistreatment, such as hanging detainees upside-down. Allegations of child trafficking by U.S. military contractors also came to light.

SURVEILLING THE POTENTIAL MESSENGER

Manning is being hailed as a hero and as a traitor. There are arguments for both. The public has a right to know about official misdeeds carried out by the government and military. But those kinds of revelations can jeopardize our defense strategy and hurt our standing in the world community.

Manning's leaks raised alarms across the government because they came from a trusted insider. In 2011, Obama issued Executive Order 13587, directing Executive Branch departments and agencies to be on guard against insider threats.

National Security Agency contractor Edward Snowden's leaks of NSA documents in 2013 only heightened official fears. As a result, government organizations have increased surveillance and are closely monitoring their employees' online activity.

With software and techniques also in use in the private sector, government agencies and contractors use computer systems that monitor when employees are accessing, copying, deleting and transferring files.

Computers' external media ports are also being watched, to detect an employee connecting a USB thumb drive that could be used to smuggle documents out of a secure system. Workers' keystrokes and other actions on their computers are being analyzed in real time to detect unauthorized activity, such as accessing restricted files or even connecting to file-sharing or social media sites.

Agencies and private companies with government contracts will also have to keep their employees' after-work lives under greater surveillance, looking for behavior or situations that might compromise government security. The effectiveness of these efforts is not yet clear.

LENIENCY OR MERCY?

Obama characterized Manning's release as a humanitarian gesture because of her personal circumstances. The day after she was sentenced, Manning revealed that she is transgender and identifies as a woman; nevertheless, she was held in a men's military prison.

The military was under increasing public and even international pressure to allow her to make a physical and biological transition – a procedure neither the military nor any U.S. prison has ever dealt with or paid for before. (She is likely to lose her military medical coverage upon her release from prison, leaving her medical care in question.)

Despite Obama's perspective, Manning's release could be viewed as an act of leniency, a signal that others might escape decades of prison time if they, too, were to violate their oaths of secrecy and reveal confidential public information. But fewer might get the chance to do so, because insiders are trusted less and being watched more.

1. What effects have Manning's leaks had on the surveillance of federal employees?

2. What arguments can be made for and against Chelsea Manning's decision to blow the whistle on the true cost of civilian casualties in the wars in Iraq and Afghanistan?

"WHY DIGITAL SECURITY MATTERS: GLOBAL TRENDS AND THE DECLINE OF NET FREEDOMS," BY DALIA HAJ-OMAR, FROM SAWTNA.NET, JUNE 24, 2015

THE SHADOW OF EDWARD SNOWDEN'S REVELATIONS

It's not a contested matter any more. Today we are living through the lowest point of optimism when it comes to the transformative power of the internet since it was first created, a little over quarter of a century ago. Perhaps nothing got us closer to this sentiment than Edward Snowden's revelations of June 2013 exposing the massive scale of the US National Security Agency's (NSA) digital surveillance and monitoring activities that targeted regular citizens, and extended beyond the US to friendly European countries.

This historic leak prompted a worldwide concern and debate about the right to digital privacy when using information communication technologies (ICTs), including the internet. As well as a debate about data localization since the NSA leaks led some countries, like Russia, Vietnam, Germany, India and others, to attempt to regulate the flow of data within their borders by requesting that international internet and technology companies store communication data pertaining to their citizens in servers inside their countries. Internet freedom advocates have expressed concern that data localization is detrimental to a free and open internet as it will make it easier for countries to spy on their citizens; may slow technological innovation; and fragment the internet by limiting global communications and e-commerce.

If any good has come from Snowden's leaks so far, it is perhaps the global pushback by civil society and some nation states and a wider recognition that the right to privacy online is a human right. In December 2013, the United Nations General Assembly passed a resolution "the right to privacy in the digital age", which urges members states to review and reverse any policies that violate the right to digital privacy. The resolution stresses that rights offline must be protected online and reminds member states that the right to privacy is included under existing international human rights law, specifically in the International Covenant on Civil and Political Rights, ratified by 167 countries so far. In March 2015 the UN Human Rights Council appointed its first ever Special Rapporteur on the Right to Privacy, whose mandate is to analyze and monitor the right to digital privacy globally; give guidance to governments and companies; and receive input from all relevant stakeholders, including civil society.

EXPANSIVE SCOPE OF INTERNET FREEDOM VIOLATIONS

Before Snowden's NSA leaks, it was usually non-democratic states that came under the spotlight for violating internet freedoms, including big violators of internet freedoms such as Cuba, Iran and China. All three countries are notorious for controlling free access to and freedom of expression on the internet through a variety of tactics that are also used by many other nations and that include but are not limited to:

1. blocking and filtering online content; 2. cyber attacks: the most aggressive being Distributed Denial of Service Attacks (DDoS); 3. blanket blocking of opposition websites, including social media; 4. shutting down the internet at times of political unrest such as protests or elections; 5. take-down requests, where bloggers are intimidated into taking down content; 6. physical attacks, including the murder of online journalists, citizen journalists and digital activists with Syria being the most deadly country for digital activists and online journalists in 2013; 7. paying commentators to manipulate discussions online; 8. introducing new laws that limit internet freedoms; and 9. monitoring and surveillance that prompts users in less democratic countries to exercise self-censorship.

INCREASE IN RESTRICTIVE LAWS AND HARSH PENALTIES

According to Freedom House's annual global survey Freedom on the Net 2014, there was a global decline in internet freedoms for the fourth year in a row in the period between May 2013 and May 2014 (the report has been published annually since 2009). "Out of 65 countries assessed, 36 have experienced a negative trajectory", with more people being detained and persecuted for their digital activities in the last year alone than in any other year.

A notable trend prevalent in both democratic and non-democratic countries, surveyed by the Freedom on the Net report, was the increase in new laws that limit internet freedoms, where 19 countries surveyed passed new laws "that increased surveillance or restricted user anonymity". In democratic countries these laws are often linked to national security concerns. This is specifically the case in France where, in reaction to the Charlie Hebdo attack of January 2015, the French National Assembly approved a law in May 2015 that would allow the country's intelligence services to monitor citizen communications without judicial oversight. French civil society has launched a campaign to raise awareness and urge citizen action against the bill.

Freedom House also notes that the penalties for online expression are often much harsher than for similar offline penalties. For example, in Ethiopia six bloggers belonging to a collective of bloggers known as the Zone 9 Bloggers have been imprisoned since April 2014, under terrorism charges, for blogging about human rights and social justice issues. Their name reflects the name of a prison in Addis Ababa that has 8 zones. Expressing the sentiment that the whole country is becoming a prison, they called themselves zone9ers, and blogged under the motto: "We Blog Because We Care", to increase the visibility of political prisoners, human rights abuses by the state and social and cultural issues.

The Middle East and North Africa saw the highest number of arrests of social media users and bloggers in recent times. Especially repressive were the countries of the Persian Gulf. Perhaps one of the most visible online and offline campaigns for an imprisoned blogger in the last year was that of the Saudi Blogger, Raif Badawi, who on May 2014 was sentenced by a criminal court in Jeddah to 10 years in prison, 1,000 lashes and a fine of more than $200,000. According to the court, Badawi had "insulted Islam" by setting up a liberal online platform that discussed religion and politics.

1. How does mass surveillance violate people's right to privacy?

2. How can limiting internet freedom be used to oppress people?

CHAPTER 6

WHAT REGULAR CITIZENS SAY

When the public is made aware of corruption and illegal activities, especially on the part of their elected officials through leaks, they must decide how to respond. Public support for whistleblowers can act as a form of protection for the whistleblower. For example, after public outcry, Chelsea Manning was removed from solitary confinement. Manning's leaks added fuel to the antiwar movement with many activists seeing her actions as morally just. Others saw Manning's leaks as treason. However, the public has another role as well and that is to act as whistleblowers if privy to injustice or corruption. Not every whistleblower is as high profile as Manning. Corruption happens in all walks of life. Citizens should be encouraged to blow the whistle on unethical or unjust activity they may observe. But in order for citizens to become whistleblowers they must feel they will be reasonably protected if they come forward.

"HACKING/JOURNALISM," BY PHILIP DI SALVO, FROM *LIMN*

Journalism and hacking are getting closer in recent times. WikiLeaks, the Snowden case and the other published "megaleaks" have blurred the boundaries between news-rooms and hackers and inspired the rise of a hybrid form of reporting, where elements historically associated with hacking are now also visibly involved in journalism. This hybridization is the result of a process of boundary-cross-ing, whose most visible manifestation is in the adoption of new technologies. For instance, reporters increasingly rely on encryption tools to protect their sources and their work. Whistleblowing cases have been where this process has taken place in the most extensive way.

Whistleblowers have always supplied investigative reporters with leaks, leads, and documents. The notable US instances from the 70s, like the Watergate and the Pentagon Papers cases, established whistleblowing-led journalism and made it mainstream and part of the popular record. The act of blowing the whistle hasn't changed much since. A substantial game changer was WikiLeaks and the digital "megaleaks" it published starting from 2010. WikiLeaks' Afghan and Iraqi War Logs, together with the Cablegate leaks, were an unprecedented novelty for journalism: they were composed of a hundred thousand documents in digital format that were leaked through encrypted channels to a hacker organization by Chelsea Manning, a US soldier turned whistleblower with cultural ties to the hacking community. When it comes to journal-istic and newsroom practices, the most disruptive change came when WikiLeaks began to partner with major news organizations to publish material; encryption played an enabling role in that whistleblowing. The WikiLeaks and journalists "consortium" represented a turning point in the relationship between journalism and hacking and it was able to put hackers and reporters at the same table, working jointly by sharing goals, skills, tools and practices. On that occasion, WikiLeaks contributed the source material and the technology, a resource that newspapers didn't have at the time, while journalists brought their editorial skills and knowledge and, moreover, access to their audiences and influence.

In 2013 the Snowden case strengthened further the connection between hackers and journalists. Whistleblower Edward Snowden had strong affinities with the hacking community; the subjects of the leak – surveillance and cybersecurity – were core issues for hackers and, once again, encryption tools played a fundamental part in facilitating communication between the source and the journalists. Allegedly, Glenn Greenwald risked losing the story of the decade by not following Snowden's request to communicate via safer channels. The debate about encryption that followed the Snowden case inspired more journalists and media outlets to adopt cybersecurity strategies and practices in order to better protect their work in times of pervasive digital surveillance. At the same time, other similar hacking-influenced instances of journalism based on digital leaks have also multiplied: Offshore Leaks (or the "Panama Papers", "Swiss Leaks" and "Luxembourg Leaks"), published by the International Consortium of Investigative Journalists (ICIJ) and the "Drone Papers", published by *The Intercept*. These cases helped set new standards for reporting on leaked material and showed the potential of a proactive attitude towards encryption.

As Baack argues (2016), digital leaks have now become normalized for contemporary journalism and, because of the recurring presence of hackers and their technology, it is possible to look at some of these instances in order to describe how journalism is becoming more like hacking. The encryption tools used by Snowden and Greenwald to communicate with one another, for instance, exemplifies how journalists and reporters are now routinely embedding traditional hacking tools within their toolbox. Pretty Good Privacy (PGP) encryption software, the Off-the-record (OTR) encryption chatting protocol, and the mobile app Signal are now commonly included in the journalism toolbox; digital security literacy is now directly associated with the duty of protecting sources in the digital era. WikiLeaks pioneered a peculiar tactic to digital whistleblowing with its own online encrypted anonymizing submission system, whose approach is now used, via the hacker-coded GlobaLeaks and SecureDrop open source software, also by several major news organizations such as *Associated Press, Washington Post, The Guardian* and *Vice*, among others. Encryption has now become a crucial strategy for reporters in need of a safe digital environment, or to apply "data disobedience" to shield their work (Brunton & Nissembaum, 2015: 62).

The adoption of encryption in journalism has created a hybridization of practices between hackers and journalists that can be described as a "trading zone" (Galison, 1997; Lewis and Usher, 2014). "Trading zones" are symbolic spaces where actors hailing from different backgrounds work with shared purposes. For hackers, encryption has always held connotations of political resistance and the stress on privacy protection and anonymity safeguards is often part of the definition of the identity of hackers as well. For journalists encryption helps protect not only themselves and their work, but also their sources, giving them robust safeguards and protection from tracking and retaliation. In their tripartite analysis, Coleman and Golub (2008) have identified "cryptofreedom" to indicate how encryption is used by hackers as one "moral expression of hacking." In the "trading zone" between hackers and journalists what is being adopted by the latter is an approach to technology—and encryption tools in particular—that wasn't at all routinized in journalism before WikiLeaks and Snowden. Charlie Beckett (2012: 32-33) defines "networked journalism" as the transformation of journalism from "a closed to an open system," where elements that were not once included in the journalism ecosystem are now being embedded in it. In recent times, "networked journalism" has been used to explain the context in which new formats of news making, new identities, and new professional boundaries have been set. Data journalism is a good example of this process, as it embodies elements – such as data analysis and data visualization – that are not defining elements of journalism per sé. Consequently, the "boundaries of journalism" have expanded (Carlson and Lewis, 2015) to the extent that tactics whose roots are not entirely in journalism – such as adopting encryption tools in our case – can now have a role in the media ecosystem and can contribute to the news-making process.

This said, the encounter of journalism with hacking can't be explained by changes in journalism alone. This hybrid "trading zone" has also been enabled by the growing process of politicization of hacking and the new political stances that emerged among hackers engaged in direct action or civil disobedience as tactics (Coleman, 2017). Politicization has become more visible especially in regards to leaks in the service of civic and public goals and with media exposure as an aim. Hackers and hacktivists have become more involved in the communication field and more interested in "work traditionally ascribed to journalists, expanding what it means to be involved in the production of news and, in the process, gaining influence over how traditional news stories and genres are constructed and circulated" (Russell, 2016: 7). This process was also helped by the "fluidity" of the hacker identity which, despite a loose acceptance of a common ethos, has always been "pliable, performative and fluid" (Fish & Follis, 2016) and consequently open to the widening of the spectrum of their activities.

According to Adrienne Russell, this hybridization is also visible in the rise of what she calls a new "media vanguard" composed of "journalists, activists, communication-technology hackers" who "are exerting significant influence in today's media environment through innovation and media competence" (2016: 9-10). At the current stage, it is important to point out how this hacking-influenced form of reporting has received differential forms of acceptance within the journalism community. It would be wrong to claim this represents a globally accepted status quo. Some news outlets, especially in the US, have embraced working with hackers and technology more explicitly and have made it the defining element of their editorial strategy: Glenn Greenwald's *The Intercept*, for instance, has put "adversarial journalism" in the field of surveillance and cyber-affairs at its core. Together with the wide adoption of encryption as a central component of its reporting, *The Intercept* has been extensively covering hacking cases, establishing a generally positive attitude towards hackers. *ProPublica* also frequently works with hackers and coders of different backgrounds, including digital security or data journalism, and has also published first-hand reporting on the Snowden documents.

Other outlets' acceptance of hacking has been far more reserved: while still covering news or documents coming from hacking cases, for instance, the *New York Times*, has been notably critical of hackers and hacktivists such as Julian Assange; and they have been more aloof than other news outlets while covering Edward Snowden (Di Salvo & Negro, 2015). The *Washington Post*, despite having reported on the Snowden files, having won a Pulitzer Prize for its own coverage of the NSA case, and being a SecureDrop adopter, called for President Obama not to pardon Snowden (*Washington Post*, 2016). Further research, and ethnographic research in particular, will help in grasping the new boundaries of journalism and how they are set, established and influenced by hacking. When it comes to digital security, encryption and source protection, for instance, the contribution of hackers is crucial for literacy, knowledge sharing and tools-crafting in the journalistic field. Moreover, hacking-influenced journalism has proven to be a catalyst for investigative reporting; some of the most interesting journalistic investigations of recent times has involved some form of hacking. For newsrooms, in times of pervasive digital surveillance, journalists are put under new threats and pressures. Being proactively ready to assist whistleblowers and sources with proper encryption tools will become increasingly urgent.

1. Since technology makes leaks easier, how has this affected journalism?

2. What is the difference between hacking and investigative journalism?

"'FAST AND FURIOUS' WHISTLEBLOWERS WELCOME EFFORT TO PROTECT OTHERS," MIRANDA LEO, FROM *CRONKITE NEWS*, FEBRUARY 25, 2015

Two men who exposed the government's failed Operation Fast and Furious gun-running probe in Phoenix said they hope a new Senate caucus can keep other whistleblowers from enduring the retaliation they faced.

Pete Forcelli and John Dodson were in Washington on Wednesday as a bipartisan group of senators introduced the Senate Whistleblowers Protection Caucus. The two men said the caucus can better implement the laws already in place that are meant to protect whistleblowers but are too easily and too often ignored by federal agencies.

"As a caucus they can act," Dodson said. "They can provide that focused beam of light on a whistleblower, on an issue, that can give them some protection that the law can't afford."

Senators in the caucus said they hope to use it to better protect whistleblowers from internal consequences and, through those efforts, encourage would-be truth-tellers to come forward without the fear of agency retaliation.

"At the end of the day, this is not about writing a law and saying your job is done. This is about the kind of ongoing oversight, the ongoing watch dog efforts the caucus really envisions," said Sen. Ron Wyden, D-Ore.

Forcelli and Dodson were working for the Bureau of Alcohol, Tobacco, Firearms and Explosives in Arizona four years ago when they reported concerns about Operation Fast and Furious. Under the probe, prosecutors and ATF agents let guns "walk" – hoping that they could trace the weapons from the straw buyers in Arizona to the cartels and kingpins in Mexico and elsewhere that they believed were organizing the otherwise illegal gun deals.

But of the roughly 2,000 weapons that walked in the investigation, many were never recovered and two were found at the scene of shootout that killed Border Patrol Agent Brian Terry near Rio Rico, Ariz., in December 2010.

The investigation into the failed operation led to the resignation of several top ATF officials as well as a vote by the House holding Attorney General Eric Holder in contempt of Congress.

Both Forcelli and Dodson said after they came forward they faced the retaliation the caucus aims to protect against.

Dodson, who used to be involved in undercover operations, said that the fallout changed his life, career and relationships dramatically.

"It's hard for me now to even remember what my life was like, it's like a dream that someone else had. A memory of how great things were and how much I loved my job, and I loved going to work and the friends that I had and the job that I thought we were doing," he said.

"I thought I was on the right team and we were doing the good deeds. And now I question all that," Dodson said. "I've lost those friends, my contacts and every position I've had with my agencies, it's gone. My entire world is different."

Forcelli said he did not face the same level of shunning and distancing from within the ATF that Dodson did, but he was still forced to move out of Arizona due to the persecution and false allegations he encountered from federal prosecutors in the state.

"In many instances there are no penalties for retaliation or making allegations against whistleblowers and I think that's something that needs to be addressed," he said.

He hopes the caucus can help fix that.

"We as people who swear an oath to the Constitution, that oath is to the people. Not to an agency, not to the government, not to a political party," Forcelli said. "People should be encouraged to come forward and tell the truth and not suffer repercussions."

1. What kind of repercussions did Dodson face after becoming a whistleblower?

2. How would a caucus help whistleblowers?

"NWAD SIGN-ON LETTER," FROM THE NATIONAL WHISTLEBLOWERS CENTER, JUNE 18, 2015

Dear Mr. President and Leaders of Congress:

The undersigned write to urge you to publicly recognize the courage of whistleblowers by supporting National Whistleblower Appreciation Day. On July 30th, 1778 at the height of the American Revolution, our Founding Fathers unanimously passed what very well may be the world's first law supporting whistleblowers and recognizing the right of all citizens to report "misconduct, frauds and misdemeanors" to the "appropriate authority." Whistleblowers are our first and best line of defense against fraud and misconduct. Every day they save the taxpayers' money, protect the public safety, and play a vital role in ensuring government and corporate accountability.

However, many Americans who have witnessed misconduct and corruption fear they will be retaliated against by their employer or unsupported by the government after risking their careers to report violations of law. Setting July 30th aside to recognize the wisdom of the Founding Fathers' vision and celebrate the accomplishments of whistleblowers will alleviate that fear. It will help transform a culture where hostility towards whistleblowers is all too common promote integrity and accountability.

We strongly commend the Senate for passing the 2013 and 2014 resolutions recognizing National Whistleblower Appreciation Day. We urge the Senate to do the same again this year and urge the House of Representatives to recognize the day as well. We also urge Congress and the President to work together to introduce legislation marking National Whistleblower Appreciation Day as a permanent day recognizing the historic actions of our Founding Fathers and celebrating the contributions of whistleblowers.

As part of the legislation we urge Congress to require the heads of each federal agency use that day as an opportunity to set the 'tone at the top,' calling public attention to the contributions whistleblowers have made to American democracy and their own agencies. The legislation should mandate that during the week upon which July 30th falls each year all federal agencies should highlight the role whistleblowers have played in their agencies to combat waste, fraud, and abuse and enforce the laws of the land.

Having the head of each federal agency publicly acknowledge the value of whistleblowers will play a critical role in changing the perception of whistleblowers. Designating July 30th as a permanent occasion to celebrate whistleblowers will create an opportunity and a platform to change a culture that all too often prevents law enforcement from learning about waste, fraud and abuse that harms the taxpayers, into one that actively encourages citizens to play a role in combating fraud and corruption. On July 30th, 1778, our Founding Fathers made it clear that bringing misconduct and abuse to light was a fundamental part of being a citizen in the new democracy. They unanimously resolved:

"That it is the duty of all persons in the service of the United States, as well as all other inhabitants thereof, to give the earliest information to Congress or any other proper authority of any misconduct, frauds or misdemeanors committed by any persons in the service of these states, which may come to their knowledge."

Our Founding Fathers foresaw that whistleblowers would play a critical role in maintaining the integrity of our democratic institutions and protecting our nation from fraud and corruption. Whistleblowers have succeeded remarkably in this role. It is time our government officially recognize the foresight of our Founding Fathers.

Respectfully submitted

1. Should there be a National Whistleblower Appreciation Day?

2. How do whistleblowers help maintain the integrity of democratic institutions?

"WORST KNOWN GOVERNMENTAL LEAK EVER IS SLOWLY COMING TO LIGHT: AGENCY MOVED NATION'S SECRET DATA TO 'THE CLOUD,'" BY RICK FALKVINGE, FROM *PRIVACY NEWS ONLINE*, JULY 21, 2017

SWEDEN'S TRANSPORT AGENCY MOVED ALL OF ITS DATA TO "THE CLOUD", APPARENTLY UNAWARE THAT THERE IS NO CLOUD, ONLY SOMEBODY ELSE'S COMPUTER. IN DOING SO, IT EXPOSED AND LEAKED EVERY CONCEIVABLE TOP SECRET DATABASE: FIGHTER PILOTS, SEAL TEAM OPERATORS, POLICE SUSPECTS, PEOPLE UNDER WITNESS RELOCATION. NAMES, PHOTOS, AND HOME ADDRESSES: THE LIST IS JUST GETTING STARTED. THE RESPONSIBLE DIRECTOR HAS BEEN FOUND GUILTY IN CRIMINAL COURT OF THE WHOLE AFFAIR, AND SENTENCED TO THE HARSHEST SENTENCE EVER SEEN IN SWEDISH GOVERNMENT: SHE WAS DOCKED HALF A MONTH'S PAYCHECK.

Many governments have had partial leaks in terms of *method* (Snowden) or *relations* (Manning) lately, but this is the first time I'm aware that the full treasure chest of every single top-secret governmental individual with photo, name, and home address has leaked. It goes to show, *again*, that governments can't even keep their most secret data under wraps — so any governmental assurances to keep *your* data safe have as much value as a truckload of dead rats in a tampon factory.

It started out with a very speedy trial where a Director General in Sweden was fined half a month's pay. Given how much the establishment has got each other's backs, this sentence was roughly equivalent to life in prison for a common person on the street, meaning they must have done something *really awful* to get not just a guilty verdict, but actually be fined half a month's salary.

On digging, it turns out the Swedish Transport Agency moved all its data to "the cloud", as managed by IBM, two years ago. Something was found amiss when the Director General of the Transport Agency, Maria Ågren, was quickly retired from her position this January — but it was only on July 6 that it became known that she was found guilty of exposing classified information in a criminal court of law. The scandal quickly escalated from there.

There's an enormous amount of data in Swedish about the overall leak scandal, but among all that data, one piece bears mentioning just to highlight the generally sloppy, negligent, and indeed criminal, attitude toward sensitive information:

Last March, the entire register of vehicles was sent to marketers subscribing to it. This is normal in itself, as the vehicle register is public information, and therefore subject to Freedom-of-Information excerpts. What was *not* normal were two things: first, that people in the witness protection program and similar programs were included in the register distributed outside the Agency, and second, when this fatal mistake was discovered, a new version without the sensitive identities was *not* distributed with instructions to destroy the old copy. Instead, the sensitive identities were *pointed out* and *named in a second distribution* with a request for all subscribers to remove these records *themselves*. This took place in open cleartext e-mail.

Take this incident and scale it up to everyday behavior at a whole agency with key responsibility for safeguarding national secrets.

At present, these databases are known to have been exposed, by moving them to "The Cloud" as if it were just a random buzzword:

The weight capacity of all roads and bridges (which is crucial for warfare, and says a lot about what roads are intended to be used as wartime airfields);

Names, photos, and home addresses of fighter pilots in the Air Force;

Names, photos, and home addresses of everybody and anybody in a police register, all of which are classified;

Names, photos, and home addresses of all operators in the military's most secret units – equivalent to the SAS or SEAL teams;

Names, photos, and home addresses of everybody in a witness relocation program or who has been given protected identity for other reasons;

Type, model, weight, and any defects of any and all government and military vehicles, including their operator, which says a ton about the structure of military support units;

the list goes on.

All of this was not just outside the proper agencies, but outside the European Union, in the hands of people who had absolutely no security clearance. All of this data can be expected to have been permanently exposed.

Let's be clear: if a common mortal had leaked this data through this kind of negligence, the penalty would be life in prison. But not when done by the government themselves. Half a month's pay was the harshest conceivable sentence.

The leak is still ongoing and can be expected to be fixed "maybe this fall, perhaps". Much of the available analysis of the leak is still in the form of fully-redacted documents from the Security Police and similar agencies.

Privacy really really *really* remains your own responsibility.

1. What should be done when information is leaked accidentally?

2. Should people be notified if personally identifiable information about them is accidentally leaked?

EXCERPT FROM "EU GEARS UP TO ATTACK WHISTLEBLOWERS WITH NEW TRADE SECRET LAWS," BY JULIA REDA, FROM *JULIA REDA*, AUGUST 4, 2016

In many of the biggest political scandals of the past months – Luxleaks, Dieselgate and now the Panama Papers – we saw **trade secret laws abused** as a shield against investigation and exposure of how corporations are harming the public good, avoiding taxes and endangering public safety. Whistleblowers find themselves fighting for their freedom in court – or in hiding. And yet, **the European Parliament is about to expand corporate secrecy and deter whistleblowing by adopting the Trade Secrets Directive**.

LEX WIKILEAKS

According to research conducted by Austrian investigative journalist Erich Moechel, preparations for the Directive **coincided with Wikileaks revelations** first making international headlines. He points out the discrepancy between the European Parliament's decision to award LuxLeaks whistleblower Antoine Deltour with the European Citizen's Prize 2015, after his revelations led to recovering several hundred million euro of tax revenue, while at the same time preparing to pass a law that will make the kind of prosecution that Antoine Deltour now faces for trade secrets disclosure in Luxembourg a norm across Europe.

The Greens/EFA, my political group in the European Parliament, will reject the Directive in the plenary vote on **Thursday April 14th**, echoing the concerns by over half a million petition signatories across Europe as well as civil society organizations including the Confederation of German Trade Unions, Corporate Europe Observatory, Syndicat National des Journalistes and Whistleblower Netzwerk e.V.

We proposed delaying the vote until the Directive can be paired with a **Whistleblower Protection Directive**, a draft for which our group will present on May 4. In rejecting this proposal, the EPP and S&D groups are deciding to press on to broaden companies' abilities to keep important information away from the public eye and deter leaks while the Panama Papers continue to be front-page news.

EFFECTS OF ADOPTING THE DIRECTIVE

1. A right to hide wrongdoing

In many member states, the Trade Secrets Directive will **broadly expand the definition** of what kind of information may be protected. The new definition (Article 2) does not exclude e.g. information about illegal or harmful activities or pending investigations into such.

It provides a floor, but not a ceiling for trade secret protection in the EU: Member states may have even further-reaching criminal law provisions. Existing criminal provisions are bound to be updated to cover the new broad definition, whereas the Directive's exceptions will not automatically apply to them.

> Example: Germany today requires companies to demonstrate a legitimate interest in what they claim as trade secrets. Only business information can be protected – ruling out protection i.e. for information about an ongoing investigation. These essential limitations would be dropped.

2. A CHILLING EFFECT ON WHISTLEBLOWING

It appears that you have had unauthorized access to proprietary documents and information taken from our company [...] We trust that you are fully aware that using information/documentation unlawfully obtained is a crime, and we will not hesitate to pursue all available criminal and civil remedies.

— Mossack Fonseca's response to the Panama Papers, 3 April 2016

The Directive will increase the ability of companies caught red-handed to **sue whistleblowers** and investigative journalists. It places the **burden of proof** of acting in the public interest on the whistleblower – and refers to the "general public interest", for which no common definition exists.

It does not preclude member states from **making whistleblowers criminals**. In January 2015, the French government attempted to introduce laws threatening 3 years in jail and a fine of €375,000 for disclosing trade secrets in anticipation of this Directive. While ultimately defeated, that attempt foreshadows the increased rigor we can expect to see in other member states.

Given the massive power imbalance between whistleblowers (usually workers) and corporations who can afford protracted legal battles, this is bound to cause a significant **chilling effect** – even after the repeated demonstrations over the last few months that society increasingly relies on insiders to expose malpractice that evades national law enforcement and democratic oversight.

Example: Edward Snowden's revelations of massive global suspicionless surveillance would likely not meet the criteria of the Directive's whistleblower exception.

3. THREATS TO PUBLIC SAFETY AND OVERSIGHT

Because the Directive makes no distinction based on the purpose for which secret information is acquired, used or disclosed, it does not just protect companies from corporate espionage, unfair competition etc., but also from **many legitimate needs to access unknown information**. Some examples:

1. **Dieselgate**: The German safety testing organisation TÜV was unable to inspect car engine software for emissions testing defeat devices because car manufacturers claimed trade secrets protection.

2. **Deadly experiment**: In a French drug trial this year, a man died. When scientists requested access to crucial data to find out what happened, the sponsoring company refused, claiming trade secret protection.

3. **Secret studies**: The EU based its controversial assessment that the active ingredient of Monsanto's Roundup herbicide (glyphosate) is "unlikely" to cause cancer – contradicting WHO findings – in part on industry-sponsored studies that are unavailable for examination by independent scientists due to trade secrets claims.

4. THREATS TO WORKERS' RIGHTS AND MOBILITY

In negotiations with the Council, an amendment was dropped that ensured knowledge gained on the job can not be classified as a trade secret. This exposes workers to the **risk of being sued by their previous employer for 6 years** after changing jobs. While the Directive does not itself introduce sanctions against the disclosure of knowledge under these circumstances, it leaves member states open to do so.

Fact: The vast majority of trade secrets lawsuits today involve companies suing former or existing employees. (Source: Corporate Europe Observatory)

REACTIONS

*We ask the Members of European Parliament to vote against this directive. It is suitable to restrict the possibilities of journalistic research, **intimidate** journalists and hinder editorial work by high cost risks.*

> —Editorial committees of ARD, ZDF, Deutschlandradio and Deutsche Welle (AGRA)

*Do you really want a society where it is impossible for the public to access information **crucial** to the public good?*

> —Antoine Deltour, LuxLeaks whistleblower and awardee of the European Citizens' Prize 2015

They transformed a legislation which should have regulated fair competition between compa-

*nies into something resembling **a blanket right to corporate secrecy**, which now threatens anyone in society who sometimes needs access to companies' internal information without their consent: consumers, employees, journalists, scientists…*

—Corporate Europe Observatory, European Network of Scientists for Social and Environmental Responsibility (ENSSER), Syndicat des Avocats de France (SAF), Syndicat National des Journalistes (SNJ), Tax Justice Network, Transparency International France, Whistleblower-Netzwerk e.V. and over 40 further NGOs

*The proposal […] **bears serious risk to consumers' and workers' interests, to the environment and to human rights**. The protection of whistleblowers – the majority of them are workers – will be insufficient […]. It is also disappointing that skills and expertise gained in the context of employment relationships can potentially be declared trade secrets.*

—Annelie Buntenbach, German Trade Unions Confederation, Member of the Executive Board

*[…] a lot of legal uncertainty still surrounds the circumstances in which investigative journalists and their sources can be sued. Faced with the prospect of having to pay compensatory damages, this uncertainty **will lead to journalists and their sources keeping valuable information to themselves**.*

—Anne Friel, Lawyer, European Aarhus Centre

The Directive coming into force would lead to a de facto **restriction of the freedom of the press** *and information at the European level*

—Cornelia Haß, Chairperson, German Journalists' Union (DJU)

Adopting a text that creates a situation where secrecy is the legal norm for companies' internal information and transparency is the exception is clear proof of the European Commission's preference towards **corporate interest over public interest**.

—Benedek Javor, Bureau of the Intergroup on Integrity Transparency Corruption and Organised Crime (ITCO)

[...]

1. Should the burden of proof be on whistleblowers or the accused?

2. What should count as a "trade secret"?

"RESEARCHERS' ANIMAL CRUELTY AT U.S. MEAT ANIMAL RESEARCH CENTER," BY KATHY BARKER, FROM SCIENTISTS AS CITIZENS, JANUARY 24, 2015

The treatment of experimental animal is not a topic many scientists are willing to talk about, other than to say that animal models are necessary for understanding human biology. With this belief and the belief that it is being done for the good of people, a critical look at the practice (and certainly not the morality) of animal experimentation is not systemically done.

Would knowing that animals are being treated extraordinarily cruelly in order to further the needs of the meat industry make a difference in considering the realities of animal experimentation?

"In Quest for More Meat Profits, U.S. Lab lets Animals Suffer," an article on page 1 of the January, 20, 2015 *New York Times*, reporter Michael Moss exposed the abuse of animals at the U.S. Meat Animal Research Center.

The U.S. Meat Animal Research Center is a federal institution in Nebraska (associated with the Univeristy of Nebraska) that centralizes animal research in the U.S. Department of Agriculture. It began about 50 years ago with the mission of helping producers of beef, pork, and lab turn a higher profit. And in the name of profit, gruesome experiments and horrible deaths are routine, as leaked by U.S. Meat Animal Research Center veterinarian scientist James Keen, who worked with the *New York Times* for a year for this article.

"Months into his new job at the center in 1989, Dr. Keen said, he got a call from a fellow worker asking him to help with a 'downed cow.'

"There was a young cow, a teenager, with as many as six bulls," he recalled. "The bulls were being studied for their sexual libido, and normally you would do that by putting a single bull in with a cow for 15 minutes. But these bulls had been in there for hours mounting her."

The cow's head was locked in a cage-like device to keep her immobile, he said. "Her back legs were broken. Her body was just torn up."

215

Dr. Keen wanted to euthanize the animal, but the scientist in charge could not be tracked down for permission. A few hours later, the cow died."

44 scientists and 73 technicians currently work at the Center. Two dozen employees were interviewed by the *New York Times*, some of whom had left the U.S. Meat Animal Research Center. Some defended the practices, but others were unhappy with the sloppy conditions in which thousands of animals have starved to death, where pain was not a deterrent to surgeries and experiments, and animals were operated on without anesthesia. These researchers, as well as technicians and other workers, spoke with the *New York Times* reporter, giving shocking testimony of callousness.

The *Times* points out that the meat business is a rough one, where even the successes are brutal: for example, 10 million piglets are crushed by their mothers every year because pigs have been breed for large litters and the mothers are kept alive so long to do nothing but reproduce. But even to other meat producers, the U.S. Meat Animal Research Center stood out for its cruel practices.

The work at the center is not subject to the provisions of the Animal Welfare Act of 1966, which protects against animal abuse, but excludes farm animals used in research to benefit agriculture. Other farm animal experimenters have sought out oversight, anyway- but not the U.S. Meant Animal Research Center.

(Nor does the Animal Welfare Act protect birds, rats, and mice bred for research, for example.)

This was an unusual article for a mainstream newspaper to print, as the machinery of justice in the USA exerts itself to protect the businesses that profit from animals, and those that expose abuse are subject to legal action. The

Animal Enterprise Terrorism Act (AETA) of 2006 forbids any action "for the purpose of damaging or interfering with the operations of an animal enterprise." Lauren Gazzola, who exposed animal mistreatment at Huntington Life Sciences, was convicted in 2006 through provisions of the weaker, pre-2006 Act because she and others ran a website that "reported on and endorsed legal and illegal protests that caused the company to lose money."

In addition, "Ag-Gag" state laws- laws that forbid photography and other exposure of conditions in the agriculture industry are on the books in several states, and are being pushed for passage in other states.

This article is in the *New York Times*, not Science or Nature or another science journal- yet. Mainstream scientific journals and organizations protect scientists' "right" to experiment on animals. The American Association for the Advancement of Science (AAAS), the Association of American Universities (AAU) ...the list is fairly endless. Perhaps scientists, and the scientific press, will one day speak out as the *New York Times* has done. Instead, they are reactive, with better treatment of animals following the exposures and actions of non-scientist activists and organizations.

When the Center heard that Keen had brought a reporter into a secure area, he was told that he would no longer be allowed in the Center. Presumably, he lost his job, and it is commendable that Keen spent a year helping the *NY Times* get this story out. But Keen had been there for 24 years, and most of the others who spoke out against the Center had already left. Fear and habit keep us silent.

Speak out when you see cruelty.

Update- Public shaming in the form of this *NY Times* article worked.

Push to Protect Farm Animals, *Science Magazine*, February 13, 2015

The U.S. Congress last week proposed new protections for farm animals used in scientific research. The move comes in response to an exposé published in *The New York Times* last month, which documented numerous cases of animal suffering and death at a Department of Agriculture facility that has been trying to create larger and more fecund farm animals for several decades. Lawmakers from both parties are backing a bill—called the AWARE Act—that would expand the scope of the Animal Welfare Act, which governs the humane treatment of laboratory animals. Farm animals are currently excluded from the act, unless they're used in biomedical research or exhibition. The new law would require closer monitoring—and more inspections—of research involving cows, pigs, and other livestock.

March 13, 2015

USDA Promises Better Oversight

New research projects have been halted at a controversial U.S. Department of Agriculture (USDA) facility, USDA Secretary Tom Vilsack announced 9 March. The agency's Meat Animal Research Center in Clay Center, Nebraska, has come under fire for allegedly causing suffering and death while trying to create larger and more fecund farm animals. Last month, Congress proposed new protections for farm animals, backing a bill called the AWARE Act that would expand the Animal Welfare Act (Science, 13 February, p. 696). A draft of a USDA report released 9 March says "no instances of animal abuse, misuse, or mistreatment were observed" at the facility, but that the center had not provided proper oversight of animal care. Vilsack said no new research would be conducted until oversight is improved. [...]

But yet, the town where the Meat Laboratory is does not seem to believe there is any cruelty happening in the Laboratory. The local TV station, in response to investigations of the lab, reported an "anti-ag agenda" on the part of the *NY Times*. Deans and cattlemen spoke up to deny any wrongdoing. Cattleman Dave Nichols had this bit of nonsense to say in response to allegations of animal cruelty: "Too many people are too far removed from producing food. Too many are poorly informed. Too many do not understand the difference between domesticated animals and their wild ancestors from 50,000 years ago. Most domesticated dogs would not last long in the wild, nor would most domesticated livestock. Not many humans would either. This is the world we live in."

So anything goes.

Yesterday on the supposedly more gentle west coast, USDA inspectors (really) reported cruelty at a research facility in Seattle: Research animals at Seattle's Children's denied care. Seattle Children's spokesperson Alyse Bernal had her own bit of irrelevance in response: "Seattle Children's Research Institute is committed to upholding the highest standards for animal research."

If you say it enough times, perhaps cruelty isn't really cruelty.

1. What role did whistleblowing play in the AWARE Act?

2. What effect did public outcry have?

CONCLUSION

In a perfect world there would be no need for whistleblowers. But as long as corruption exists there will be a need for people willing to report unethical or illegal wrong doings. While not every whistleblower acts with good intentions, many do. Whistleblowers usually feel compelled to come forward out of a sense of moral obligation or a want to protect others from harm. Unfortunately, many whistleblowers are met with harsh retaliation for coming forward.

Many government officials think that having internal avenues to report wrongdoings are sufficient to address the needs of whistleblowers. However, academics and journalists have found that reports made to internal channels often went uninvestigated and ignored. Because corruption usually comes from those in power, whistleblowers often find the media is their only outlet for having an impact. With media attention the public can become informed and hold poor actors accountable for their actions.

This puts a great deal of pressure on media organizations to vet the validity of leaked information they've been given. Journalists must understand not only the effect the information could have on the public but the motives of their source. Once journalists decide to report on leaked information they must provide the public with the necessary context to understand the leaked information.

When it comes to whistleblowers the public must be ready to support those who are trying to bring injustice to light. Promoting a culture in which whistleblowers are celebrated for ending corruption and legally protected from retaliation helps strengthen our businesses and democracy.

BIBLIOGRAPHY

Advox. "On 1st Anniversary of Snowden Revelations, World Governments Urged to End Mass Surveillance" *Advox*, June 4, 2014. https://advox.globalvoices.org/2014/06/05/on-1st-anniversary-of-snowden-revelations-world-governments-urged-to-end-mass-surveillance.

Alvarez, Alayna. "Truth and Consequences: Lessons from World-Com." *Texas Enterprise*, June 12, 2013. http://www.texasenterprise.utexas.edu/2013/06/12/workplace/truth-and-consequences-lessons-worldcom.

Austin, Janet. "Canada Offers Australia a Blueprint for Protecting and Motivating Corporate Whistleblowers." *The Conversation*, July 2, 2017. https://theconversation.com/canada-offers-australia-a-blueprint-for-protecting-and-motivating-corporate-whistleblowers-80062.

Barker, Kathy. "Researchers' Animal Cruelty at U.S. Meat Animal Research Center." *Scientists as Citizens*, January 24, 2015. http://scientistsascitizens.org/2015/01/24/researchers-animal-cruelty-at-u-s-meat-animal-research-center.

Bremer, Paul L. "Order 59: Protection and Fair Incentives for Government Whistleblowers." *Wikisource*, June 1, 2004. https://en.wikisource.org/wiki/Order_59:_Protection_and_fair_Incentives_for_Government_Whistleblowers.

Burke Robertson, Cassandra. "When is a Leak Ethical?" *The Conversation*, June 12, 2017. https://theconversation.com/when-is-a-leak-ethical-79100.

Currier, Cora. "Charting Obama's Crackdown on National Security Leaks." *ProPublica*, July 30, 2013. https://www.propublica.org/article/sealing-loose-lips-charting-obamas-crackdown-on-national-security-leaks.

Currier, Cora. "Classified Confusion: What Leaks Are Being Investigated, and What's the Law on Leaks?" *ProPublica*, July 2, 2012. https://www.propublica.org/article/classified-confusion-what-leaks-are-being-investigated-and-whats-the-law-on.

Dans, Enrique. "WikiLeaks, the CIA and the Sad Reality of the World." Enrique Dans at *Medium*, March 8, 2017. https://medium.com/enrique-dans/wikileaks-the-cia-and-the-sad-reality-of-the-world-9abf93643a3c.

Di Salvo, Philip. "Hacking/Journalism." *Limn*, Volume 8. Accessed January 19, 2018. https://limn.it/hackingjournalism.

Dunn, Alix and Ruth Miller. "Responsible Data Leaks and Whistleblowing." Responsible Data Forum, October 20, 2016. https://responsibledata.io/2016/10/20/responsible-data-leaks-and-whistleblowing.

"18 USC 798-Disclosure of Classified Information." US Government Publishing Office, January 3, 2012. https://www.gpo.gov/fdsys/granule/USCODE-2011-title18/USCODE-2011-title18-partI-chap37-sec798.

Elliott, Justin and Theodoric Meyer. "Claim on 'Attacks Thwarted' by NSA Spreads Despite Lack of Evidence." *ProPublica*, October 23, 2013. https://www.propublica.org/article/claim-on-attacks-thwarted-by-nsa-spreads-despite-lack-of-evidence.

Falkvinge, Rick. "Worst Known Governmental Leak Ever is Slowly Coming to Light: Agency Moved Nation's Secret Data to 'The Cloud'." *Privacy News Online*, July 21, 2017. https://www.privateinternetaccess.com/blog/2017/07/swedish-transport-agency-worst-known-governmental-leak-ever-is-slowly-coming-to-light.

Fargo, Anthony. "How Should You Read Unnamed Sources and Leaks?" *The Conversation*, January 23, 2017. https://theconversation.com/how-should-you-read-unnamed-sources-and-leaks-71214.

Fields, Jeffrey. "What is Classified Information, and Who Gets to Decide?" *The Conversation*, May 16, 2017. https://theconversation.com/what-is-classified-information-and-who-gets-to-decide-77832.

Forno, Richard and Anupam Joshi. "The WikiLeaks CIA Release: When Will We Learn?" *The Conversation*, March 8, 2017. https://theconversation.com/the-wikileaks-cia-release-when-will-we-learn-74226.

Goel, Sanjay. "Is Part of Chelsea Manning's Legacy Increased Surveillance?" *The Conversation*, January 20, 2017. https://theconversation.com/is-part-of-chelsea-mannings-legacy-increased-surveillance-71607.

GovTrack Insider. "Two Bills Congress is Considering May Create Future Edward Snowdens." *GovTrack Insider*, July 5, 2016. https://govtrackinsider.com/two-bills-congress-is-considering-may-create-future-edward-snowdens-ac3f530126e0.

Haj-Omar, Dalia. "Why Digital Security Matters: Global Trends and the Decline of Net Freedoms." *Sawtna*, June 24, 2015. http://sawtna.net/why-digital-security-matters-global-trends-and-the-decline-of-net-freedoms.

Hintz, Arne. "Whistleblowers and Leak Activists Face Powerful Elites in Struggle to Control Information." *The Conversation*, April 6, 2016. https://theconversation.com/whistleblowers-and-leak-activists-face-powerful-elites-in-struggle-to-control-information-57368.

Kelly, Anthony. "10 Ways Movements Can Encourage and Support Whistleblowers." *Waging Non-Violence*, March 23, 2017. https://wagingnonviolence.org/feature/10-ways-support-whistleblowers.

Krüger, Franz. "Ethical Journalism: What To Do - And Not To Do - With Leaked Emails." *The Conversation*, June 11, 2017. https://theconversation.com/ethical-journalism-what-to-do-and-not-to-do-with-leaked-emails-79211.

Lemieux, Frederic. "Why Trump's White House Leaks" *The Conversation*, May 16, 2017. https://theconversation.com/why-trumps-white-house-leaks-77651.

Leo, Miranda "'Fast and Furious' Whistleblowers Welcome Effort to Protect Others." *Cronkite News*, February 25, 2015. http://cronkitenewsonline.com/2015/02/fast-and-furious-whistleblowers-welcome-senate-push-to-protect-others.

National Whistleblower Center. "NWAD Sign-On Letter." June 18, 2015. https://www.whistleblowers.org/storage/docs/nwad%20sign-on%20letter.pdf.

OSHA. "Your Rights as a Whistleblower." Occupational Safety and Health Administration (OSHA), US Department of Labor. Accessed January 19, 2018. https://www.osha.gov/OshDoc/data_General_Facts/whistleblower_rights.pdf.

Reda, Julia. "EU Gears Up to Attack Whistleblowers With New Trade Secret Laws." *Julia Reda*, August 4, 2016. https://julia-reda.eu/2016/04/trade-secrets-whistleblowers.

Rifkin, Jesse. "A Loophole in Whistleblower Protection Would Be Closed with the Follow the Rules Act." *GovTrack Insider*, June 14, 2017. https://govtrackinsider.com/a-loophole-in-whistleblower-protection-would-be-closed-with-the-follow-the-rules-act-87a3815cf8b2.

Rodriguez, Katitza. "Looking Back One Year After The Edward Snowden Disclosures - An International Perspective." The Electronic Frontier Foundation, May 15, 2014. https://www.eff.org/deeplinks/2014/05/looking-back-one-year-after-edward-snowden-disclosures-international-perspective.

Rumsey, Matt "Senate Launches Bipartisan Whistleblower Protection Caucus." The Sunlight Foundation, February 26, 2015. https://sunlightfoundation.com/2015/02/26/senate-launches-bipartisan-whistleblower-protection-caucus.

Simon, Jeremy. "Knowing When to Blow the Whistle." *Texas Enterprise*, June 10, 2013. http://www.texasenterprise.utexas.edu/2013/06/10/leadership/knowing-when-blow-whistle.

Susca, Margot. "From the Pentagon Papers to Trump: How the Government Gained the Upper Hand Against Leakers."

The Conversation, June 15, 2017. https://theconversation.com
/from-the-pentagon-papers-to-trump-how-the-government-
gained-the-upper-hand-against-leakers-79159.

Tippett, Elizabeth C. "Why Companies Like Wells Fargo Ignore
Their Whistleblowers – At Their Peril." *The Conversation*,
October 24, 2016. https://theconversation.com/why-companies
-like-wells-fargo-ignore-their-whistleblowers-at-their
-peril-67501.

Tofel, Richard. "Why WikiLeaks' 'War Logs' Are No Pentagon
Papers." *ProPublica*, July 26, 2010. https://www.propublica.org
/article/why-wikileaks-war-logs-are-no-pentagon-papers.

Valencia, Robert. "Why Would Edward Snowden Want to Go to
Ecuador?" *Advox*, June 8, 2013. https://advox.globalvoices
.org/2013/07/08/why-would-edward-snowden-want-to-go-to-
ecuador.

Vitka, Sean. "Getting Secrecy Out of Science." The Sunlight
Foundation, May 22, 2014. https://sunlightfoundation
.com/2014/05/22/getting-secrecy-out-of-science.

Waldman, Annie. "Who's Regulating For-profit Schools? Execs
From For-profit Colleges." *ProPublica*, February 26, 2016.
https://www.propublica.org/article/whos-regulating-for-profit
-schools-execs-from-for-profit-colleges.

Wang, Marian. "Watch Out, Whistleblowers: Congress and Courts
Move to Curtail Leaks." *ProPublica*, May 12, 2011. https://www
.propublica.org/article/watch-out-whistleblowers-congress-
and-courts-move-to-curtail-leaks.

Wikimedia Foundation. "Wikimedia Whistleblower Policy." Wikimedia Foundation. Accessed January 19, 2018. https://wikime-
diafoundation.org/wiki/Whistleblower_policy.

CHAPTER NOTES

CHAPTER 5: WHAT THE MEDIA SAY

"HACKING/JOURNALISM" BY PHILIP DI SALVO

Baack, Stefan. (2016). "What big data leaks tell us about the future of journalism – and its past." *Internet Policy Review – Journal on Internet Regulation*.

Beckett, Charlie. (2012). *WikiLeaks. News in the Networked Era*. Cambridge: Polity Press.

Brunton, Finn & Nissenbaum, Helen. (2015). *Obfuscation. A User's Guide for Privacy and Protest*. Cambridge, MA: The MIT Press.

Carlson, Matt & Lewis, Seth. C. (eds.). (2015). *Boundaries of Journalism. Professionalism, Practices and Participation*. London: Routledge.

Coleman, Gabriella & Golub, Alex. (2008). "Hacker practice: Moral genres and the cultural articulation of liberalism." *Anthropological Theory*, 8(3): 255-277.

Coleman, Gabriella. (2017). "From Internet Farming to the Weapons of the Geek". *Current Anthropology*, vol. 58(15): 91-103.

Di Salvo, Philip & Negro, Gianluigi. (2015). "Framing Edward Snowden: A comparative analysis of four newspapers in China, United Kingdom and United States." *Journalism*, 17(7): 805-822.

Fish, Adam & Follis, Luca. (2016). "Gagged and Doxed: Hacktivism's Self-Incrimination Complex". *International Journal of Communication*, 10: 3281–3300.

Galison, Peter. (1997). *Image & logic: A Material Culture of Microphysics*. Chicago: The University of Chicago Press.

Lewis, Seth. C., & Usher, Nikki. (2014). "Code, collaboration, and the future of journalism: a case study of the Hacks/Hackers global network." *Digital Journalism*, 2(3): 383-393.

Russell, Adrienne. (2016). *Journalism as Activism. Recoding Media Power*. Cambridge: Polity.

Washington Post. (2016). "No pardon for Edward Snowden." *The Washington Post*, September 17.

GLOSSARY

classified—Confidential or secret information.

compliance—Cooperation or obedience.

corruption—Dishonest proceedings.

cyberattack—An attempt to gain access to or damage a computer or computer system.

disclosures—To make information known.

encryption—To protect a message from being read by unintended parties.

espionage—The act or practice of spying.

fraud—A trick usually used for monetary gain.

hacker—A person who uses computer skills to circumvent the security of other machines or networks.

mass surveillance—Using technology to spy on the activities of large groups of people.

misconduct—Improper behavior.

retaliation—To return like for like.

transparency—When dealings are not hidden from the public.

unethical—Lacking in moral principals.

whistleblower—A person who informs on the corruption or wrong doing of others.

FOR MORE INFORMATION

FURTHER READING

Alford, C. Fred. *Whistleblowers: Broken Lives and Organizational Power*. Ithaca, NY: Cornell University Press, 2001.

Bowman, James S. *Public Service Ethics: Individual and Institutional Responsibilities*. Los Angeles, CA: Sage, 2014.

Coleman, Gabriella. *Hacker, Hoaxer, Whistleblower, Spy: The Many Faces of Anonymous*. New York, NY: Verso, 2014.

Devine, Tom, and Tarek F. Maassarani. *The Corporate Whistleblower's Survival Guide: A Handbook for Committing the Truth*. San Francisco, CA: Berrett-Koehler, 2011.

Ellsberg, Daniel. *Secrets: A Memoir of Vietnam and the Pentagon Papers*. New York, NY: Penguin, 2003.

Goodman, Melvin A. *Whistleblower at the CIA: An Insider's Account of the Politics of Intelligence*. San Francisco, CA: City Lights, 2017.

Kohn, Stephen. *Whistleblower Law: A Guide to Legal Protections for Corporate Employees*. Westport, CT: Praeger, 2004.

Lipman, Frederick D. *Whistleblowers: Incentives, Disincentives, and Protection Strategies* (Wiley Corporate F&A). Hoboken, NJ: Wiley, 2012.

Martin Kohn, Stephen. *The New Whistleblower's Handbook: A Step-By-Step Guide To Doing What's Right And Protecting Yourself*. Gulford, CT: Lyons, 2017.

Sheehan, Neil et al. *The Pentagon Papers: The Secret History of the Vietnam War*. New York, NY: Racehorse, 2017.

WEBSITES

The National Whistleblower Center
whistleblowers.org
This nonprofit law firm provides legal assistance and support to whistleblowers. Its website features a blog, resources, attorney referrals, and ways to take action in support of leakers.

WhistleblowersUK
www.wbuk.org
This nonprofit organization aims to support whistleblowers around the world. It provides news, advice, and other information and resources on its website.

INDEX

ABOUT THE EDITOR

Rita Santos has written several books for children and young adults and edited many books for adults. She earned a master's of science in publishing from Pace University. When she's not writing or editing she loves traveling. Her greatest adventure so far was meeting sloths at the Sloth Sanctuary in Costa Rica. She is also a debt activist, advocating for the rights of student and medical debtors. Rita lives in New York City with her family and her cat, Aaron Purr.